THE GLASS IN MY THROAT

THE GLASS IN MY THROAT

B.R. White

To order additional copies of this book, contact:
Xlibris Corporation
1-888-795-4274
www.Xlibris.com
Orders@Xlibris.com
26171

CONTENTS

Because you have obeyed my command to persevere, I will protect you from the great time of testing that will come upon the whole world to test those who belong to this world . . .

—*Revelation 3:10*

ACKNOWLEDGEMENTS

First and foremost, I would like to acknowledge both my wife Denise and my mother Sadie for listening collectively over the past twenty years as I sounded off (many times in frustration) on the constant issues and roadblocks I have experienced as a black technology executive making my way through corporate America. I also want to give my heartfelt acknowledgment to my brother Darryl, who also listened to my frustration over the years and was also the first family author with his book *You and Your Credit*. He offered me inspiration to being patient and taking my time to explain my experiences.

As a frequent traveler between Philadelphia and New York, I would also like to thank radio personality Wendy Williams, whom I don't know personally, of WBLS in New York and Power99 in Philadelphia for giving me an extra push to make something like this happen by putting herself out there personally with her first book *Wendy's Got the Heat*.

The most important acknowledgment goes to my sons Brandon (nine) and Evan (seven) who inspired me to remember through their innocence that it is necessary for us as a people to share information to help the next generation. This book is dedicated to both my sons as an account of my journey though corporate America and how, on many occasions, I survived regardless of the craziness going on around me. I hope the information one day will help my sons, and possibly others, in their quest to become black executives in corporate America or entrepreneurs if their hearts lead them in that direction. Our struggles are not over, and the more we all understand this, the greater the opportunity for success.

INTRODUCTION

I've always been anal in my approach to anything in life. When I graduated from high school in low-income status, I realized I knew nothing about what it would really take to be successful in a career. As I moved through life, I made it a point to document and track all or most of my experiences for the purpose of telling my kids and others how I made it and what my experiences were. This book is a twenty-year collection of insights of my personal journey which began in a neighborhood located in Yonkers, New York, once called the bucket of blood, and concludes with my feet kicked up on my corporate corner office desk in New Jersey. *The Glass in My Throat* is not sexy or full of international intrigue. *The Glass in My Throat* was written for African Americans (from a black man's perspective) who really want to examine the good and the bad realities associated with busting through the many challenges to be faced along the road to corporate success.

The Glass in My Throat is a metaphor I created to describe my current status as an executive. In a nutshell, the book describes how I have cracked and partially climbed through the glass ceiling such that I have been enjoying life in the executive suite. However, while I have made it into the executive suite, my mouth and throat are full of glass because I am unable to completely pull myself above the glass ceiling into the next executive level, which is full of *unbelievable* financial success. Do not assume that my being stuck where I am is not rewarding. Where I am is well into the six digits, and living quite well. However, the final level is that elusive superexecutive status where homes come with seven-plus bedrooms and bonuses and stock are into the millions. Becoming a superexecutive is not a level "I need" to survive and move on with my life. My issue at this point is solely about the consistent processes and roadblocks put in place for African Americans to make it nearly impossible to reach the superexecutive level. In most nonpublic, public, midsized, and large corporations, the number of African Americans you see at the top of these corporations are *still* practically nonexistent.

The Glass in My Throat discusses issues all black people should understand if their goal is to achieve corporate or entrepreneurial success. This book covers my firsthand experiences associated with the effects of ghetto or low-income life, doing poorly in high school, the corporate interview process, and many other topics. While this book is totally factual, it does not name names for the purpose of focusing in on a particular company or person. In the end, their names are totally irrelevant. What is important is how crafty you have to become as a black person to deal with the many biases and preferences in many corporations, which are constructed with dynamically changing roadblocks, on-the-fly rules, and processes to ensure most blacks attempting to shatter the glass ceiling get stuck with "glass in their mouth!" Hopefully some of the notes from my journey will give you extra information you can utilize to reach your goals by either not making the same mistakes or recognizing patterns when certain situations occur.

The Glass in My Throat was created in two parts. Part 1 gives you an outline of what my journey encompassed and how I used all the tools I had at my disposal to survive and prevail. Part 2 is a summary section I call "cookbooks." Each cookbook is my personal recommendation regarding high school, college, and preparing for the executive ranks. The cookbooks offer an overall strategy and reference to being successful in each of the areas. The cookbooks represent information I wish was offered to me earlier in my life from a black perspective. I believe *The Glass in My Throat* should be read by every black male and female (and their parents) just prior to entering high school and college if possible. If you have already graduated, this book can be read at any time to provide insight to the realities of the corporate environment for African Americans.

CHAPTER 1

The Beginning—The Baggage That Is Us

I have read many books over the years, and I find it somewhat insulting when an overweight person writes a diet book and is still overweight or an average Joe writes a book about getting rich and still works a mediocre nine-to-five job. Since my reason for writing this book is to offer some information to black men and women about surviving the block and moving up the corporate executive ladder, I feel it is necessary to give a short historical overview of who I am and the early obstacles I had to overcome. In short, this section outlines my "props" to discuss this topic.

The earliest memory I have of my childhood is being two or three years old and sitting in a dark room, doing absolutely nothing for hours while being taken care of by a large black woman in Harlem named Mamie (little Sista'). I remember it being the most boring place on earth and waiting for the sun to go down through a window I could see at the end of a long projects apartment hallway. For whatever reason, my older brother Darryl was not there with me, making the wait that more unbearable. I remember my mom coming in to pick me up and then getting in a car to head home to Yonkers, New York. I don't remember much else about my time spent in Harlem other than it being very noisy and dirty. Except for me being born in Yonkers, New

York, everyone in my immediate family was born in Charleston, South Carolina. My father was seven years older than my mother, and he decided to drop out of high school after the eleventh grade. Apparently, when my father moved to the eleventh grade, the national school system created the twelfth grade, which meant my father would have had to attend high school another year. He refused to do so and simply never returned after his eleventh-grade year. In all honesty, I may have reacted the same way if a thirteenth year was added to my high-school requirements.

My mother, for as long as I could remember, worked in the Yonkers school system, working with special-education kids for low pay but much personal satisfaction. I remember my mom trying to attend a local college, but I think the interpersonal turmoil of leaving my brother and me in the car while she attended classes for a few hours destroyed her determination to continue, and she eventually stopped going. I am sure if she had continued, she would have easily graduated. My mother has always been extremely intelligent and book smart. Around age seven or eight, I remember my brother and me taking trips with my father to Harlem from Yonkers. We made the trip at least every weekend and sometimes during weeknights. I remember going "around town" with my father who, in retrospect, would be considered a street hustler. Everyone in Harlem knew my father, and most called him by his nicknames, which were "Snooky" and "The Dude." While not a high-school graduate or skilled with higher levels of math, my father was better than any licensed accountant when it came to managing cash and budgets. My mom's job did not bring in much money, which was meant to take care of the family needs; my father had to fill in the blanks with real hard (tax-free) cash. Since my dad was not one to get a regular job, he hustled like there was no tomorrow. I remember, on one occasion, it being very cold outside. My father was on the street corner (with my brother and me standing by his side) selling cheap dolls for little girls and knockoff Hush Puppies shoes, which would be considered today's dollar-store quality products. We were also selling cheap ladies' shoes and other types of crap. It being Harlem, people always bought stuff as long as they felt they were getting a deal. For hours we did this, and I remember acquiring a hatred for my father for making us do this in the freezing cold for hours at a time.

Over the years, my brother and I traveled all over Harlem, hustling with my father. All the while, my mother had to peddle the same crap to people at her school to bring in extra money. On so many late evening and weekend outings, my father would take my brother and me out with him to Harlem for late-evening-hour hustles. He would parade us around with him, telling people we were his sons (like a proud rooster) as he headed off into a multitude of back rooms for discussions. Sometimes my brother and I would wait around for hours before we would ever see him again. We would fall asleep for what seem to be a hundred times over just to beat the boredom of sitting at the table of a social club or in the backseat of the car. While waiting, we witnessed many women giving professionals in the alleys, as well as vicious fights on the streets.

Over time, our trips to Harlem began to dwindle down. My brother and I settled down to a regular life in Yonkers. The area we resided in Yonkers was called the Bucket of Blood. I don't know how it acquired that name, but it was basically Ravine Avenue, which was at the bottom of all the Yonkers hills adjacent to the railroad tracks and Hudson River. While I lived in Yonkers for eighteen years, my most vivid memory is of a childhood friend who died on the train tracks one weekend afternoon. I was not there when he died from falling and hitting his head on

the tracks, but it occurred just a few moments after I left. When
I returned to see the ambulance removing his body from the
tracks, it was devastating. I will never forget the vision because it
was my first experience with the death of someone I knew. Later
the next summer, some close friends and I decided to cross the
railroad tracks over to the Hudson River and play on what was
considered an uncultured beach. It was a very hot summer, and
the water did not seem as dirty as it normally looked. After a few
hours of playing around, we decided to take our shoes off and
play around the edge of the water. As the story goes, one idiot
dare turned into another, and my best friend and I (who could
not swim) found ourselves shoulder deep in the water on a beach
not approved for beach activity. A few moments later, we were
both drowning and fighting for our lives for what seemed like
hours. I could hear my heart pounding through my chest as I
realized I was going to die.

As we reached the final moments of our struggle for life, a few
large rocks came out of nowhere and allowed us to kick off in
the direction of the beach. We sat on the beach for a moment
and never talked about it again. This moment gave me a profound
appreciation to get all I can out of life.

A couple of years later, I went through my "want to be a thug"
phase. I wanted to be a member of a thug group and hang with
the crowd. Although I was an A student and was known for
being smart and being a pretty straight kid, I wanted to have
some level of edge to my persona with the guys and girls in the
hood also. To satisfy this quest, I remember joining a group (gang)
called the Little Aces. Compared to what gangs are today, ours
was nothing in comparison but still not a good thing. I ran around
with a crowd of guys whom everyone came to know because of
their mischief and occasional bad deeds. I never went along with

anything that seemed too far on the edge or hurting anyone. It seemed like a great balance until one bad Friday night. The problems began with a shirts-and-skins basketball game (older guys who were members of a gang called the Black Pearls) that ended with an argument. Somehow, a fight broke out with two guys in the Black Pearls and some other roughneck thug neighborhood guy. When the dust cleared, somebody was cut with a straight razor. I don't remember who cut who, but I do remember his chest peeling down to his waist like an orange and the yelling and blood as he ran down the street. After experiencing that, all I wanted was out of the Little Aces. Before I could bolt out of the group, later that evening, we went on a stroll to an area a bit beyond home turf. We were beyond Getty Square in Yonkers and ran into another group of guys (from another gang). I think we all were so shaken from watching the bloody fight just a few hours earlier in the day; in unison, we made a beeline to another area after seeing our adversaries. On the way home, we realized we were followed. As we approached an abandoned area near Warburton Avenue and Point Street in Yonkers, it was apparent something was going to go down. The fight itself was surreal. I remember throwing punches and hitting people all over the place, but I don't remember being punched. Immediately after feeling like a mean S.O.B. and tagging punks repeatedly, everything went black. When I woke up, I realized I was hit with a brick along with a few others and was awaken by some passersby along with a few other guys from the Little Aces. After getting about eight stitches in my head, I realized I had to make some changes.

The Little Aces and the consequences from it taught me how to be my own man and make my own path. I spent the rest of my years getting great grades, playing music, working for a congressman, becoming a track star, and graduating from high

school. At least if you knew me then, that is the picture painted
for you by me and my family.

The truth of the matter is, I was all those things outside the
home, but inside the home, life was drastically different. When I
was around twelve years old or so, life started getting better. My
father hustled his way to own a store in Harlem (Luke's Thrift
Shop), and we began to live a bit better. As with all low-income
families, some were getting by, some were poor, and some were
dirt-poor. As the thrift shop became a reality, we were on the
poor track moving on to the getting-by track. I remember
spending much time waiting on lines with my mother and brother
at the armory on Warburton Avenue in Yonkers and getting free
government products such as cheese, bread, and other such items.
I remember going on and off welfare to get some extra survival
money and occasionally still selling shoes and other such items
on the weekend in Harlem. Sometime around 1974 or 1975, I
remember things just getting better at home financially. We got
better clothes; my father was driving a better car; the dilapidated
three-family home we lived in was purchased by my father, and
we started to fix it up and collect rent. My brother and I (through
the suggestion of my father) started an ice-water stand in the
front of the house, and the business itself became legendary in
our area of the hood. We had lines of fifty-plus people on some
days and made excellent money. It was great!

One day in local community center, there was a special police
awareness day with a focus on avoiding drugs and staying in school.
During the session, the police demonstrated the activities of drug
dealers and their tools of the trade along with various cutting
(drug mixture) substances used with the street selling of cocaine
and other such drugs. During the demonstration, they discussed
activities such as mass money counting and code names for

everything being done. While I attended the class, I had no interest in the topic and was primarily messing around with my friends and not paying attention. Sometime later, we had a small school function, and my father came by to pick me up because my mother could not get off work. During the quick hellos and goodbyes, to my surprise, my father gave a name that I never heard before. I asked my father about the false name he gave and was basically blown off. I doubt he ever cared or understood how confusing and personally hurtful that was to me, but all I saw and felt was my father denying his family. One week later, at about 2 a.m., my father came home and stomped up the stairs the way he normally did. He called my brother and me into the kitchen (along with my mother), and we began our nightly routine as we normally did. It was not until I was twenty minutes into the process that I realized there were bottles called dextrose and lactose and scales, and my mother was counting large sums of money along with my brother. I had a V-8 moment as I realized what was going on and simply thought, oh, damn! My father is dealing drugs!

As time went by, our trips to his Harlem thrift store picked up in frequency and we realized the business was only a front to store his powdery goods. As the trips became more frequent, my brother and I found ourselves waiting in the car again for hours. One of the last things I remember was a fight between two men in which one guy's head was slammed into the top of a fire hydrant, and he later died. At a young age, my brother and I learned just how nasty street life really was and the dangers of playing the game. In addition to the issues we were already dealing with, my brother and I came to understand why we were waiting for hours at a time. While we thought it was only about Super Fly deals he transacted, we later also met a number of women all over Harlem through my father. We also came to realize we had a number of half brothers and half sisters all over New York and Connecticut. I have no idea where they are today, nor do I remember many of their names.

When I was around sixteen years of age, I remember my father losing a drastic amount of weight and not talking very much at all. Overall, his not talking was nothing new to me and was probably due to all his Camel smoking; I assumed he had cancer or something. Toward the end of the year, my father began to look healthy again. It turned out some feds or local police recorded a drug deal he was involved in, and he was out on bail. He was losing weight because the tapes were solid evidence, and they had a snitch that turned him in. In the end, late one night, the police's star witness (the snitch) was gunned down, and my father went free and started gaining weight again after all the worrying was over. In all honesty, if my father had gone to jail at that time and I never saw him again, I am not sure I would have cared. During the time I knew my father, I never received a hug, "that a boy," a personal visit to any of my sporting events, or any concern about my homework or anything else. We never did anything together that was not about his interest or the interest of his street customers. The biggest event (bonding if you will) between my father, my brother, and me was washing his car. When we were washing his car, it was the only time we felt as if we mattered in any way from a father-and-son standpoint. The only other moment was when we emptied his car of hot goods he acquired off the street for us to wear, eat, or store. Many of our home goods were hot off the street, and that was just a way of life I came to understand.

As my graduation from high school approached, our house burned down to the ground in Yonkers. By this time, my brother was at Howard University, and it was mostly my mother, grandmother, and I living in Yonkers. I remember going out to the store on that freezing, cold night, and everything looked fine. When I returned, I entered our home and smelled smoke. We called the fire department, and by the time they arrived, I found a small contained fire in the basement in a small bunch of leaves in a corner. Just as I was going to pour water on the flames, the fire department shuffled me out, and one hour later (just as we thought the fire was out), the whole house went up in flames. We were out on the street! What came next that evening changed my view forever concerning friendships and relationships. As I sat outside, waiting for my father in my rusty car, looking out for what was left of our belongings, many of the people I knew in the neighborhood raided the rubble and began stealing my family's stuff. I realized then what type of friends I had in the hood. I think that because the drug money gave us a better quality of life (materially), a hatred for us existed. In one night, most of the people I grew up with changed from being longtime friends to thieving bastards I was forced to run off with a stick away from the half-burned stereo and cash my father kept in a duffel bag in the basement. Before the night was over, I experienced my last and final outrage. As my mother and grandmother stood in the cold trying to deal with what occurred, the Red Cross ignored helping them and focused on giving coffee and blankets to the police and firemen who were wet from the hoses and freezing cold. It was a night of inhumanity I will never forget.

The next morning, my mother and grandmother moved to Queens, but I kept residence with a friend in Yonkers in order to complete graduation. My last year was very difficult. On some nights, I drove to Queens to be with my mother, which meant that to get to school, I had to drive twenty-six miles through multiple highways at least two to three days a week. I later graduated from Gorton High School in Yonkers and moved on to the University of Maryland.

In December of 1981, while I was studying for the finals, the news came that my father had been murdered in one of his storefronts. While in his "social spot," he and a friend were ambushed on Eighth Avenue in Harlem near 135th Street. His friend was decapitated via two shotgun blasts to the head while tied to a chair, and my father was stabbed with scissors and shot to death while trying to fight. He was found on the floor by the police near the rear entrance. It appeared he was still alive after the assailants left and tried to make it out the back but died on the way. What is most interesting about his demise is that by simple dumb luck, I took a surprise trip to New York to visit my mother and because she wanted to make me breakfast before I returned to college, my mother decided not to go with my father to Harlem as he requested. If I had not returned home, the odds are my mother would have gone with him to Harlem and she too would have died in the assault.

Shortly after his murder, all hell broke loose by street thugs trying to avenge my father's murder. The atmosphere was so bad that a very good friend of mine who lived off Getty Square was accosted at gunpoint while going home but was not shot or robbed. At this point, I had no idea if this was a warning to not seek revenge or just a random event. I truly believed all my friends were in danger because of me and the people thinking that whenever I returned to New York, I was trying to avenge my father's death. From that point on, for the next four years, I broke off all contact with many old friends in New York until things calmed down. Eventually they did, but I never returned to New York for more than a day or a few hours at a time.

While my father was a poor excuse for a dad, he had a good heart and often gave away money to help many people especially those in our immediate family. I personally found it contradictory when our churchgoing Southern relatives demonstrated their dislike for my father intensely but accepted his money if they were in a bind. I found it interesting that my father knew they hated him, but he would never refuse to help if things got tough. When my dad was killed, no emotional support of any kind was offered to my family from our relatives in South Carolina. We received only a couple of sympathy cards from my Uncle Carl and Aunt Shirley. The fact that my mother received no support of any kind was no surprise to me because as a child I don't remember anyone (my mother's brothers or sisters) calling from South Carolina just to shoot the breeze or say hello to my brother and me. I was sad for my mother because she deserved better from her siblings. God has taught me to forgive this behavior and move on, but the forgetting part is not as easy to execute.

This chapter only gives the highlights of what I have seen growing up in Yonkers and Harlem. Other details are much more gruesome (especially from my brother's viewpoint since he was older) but not necessary to explain any further. My reason for including all this information is to basically say that we all have a story to tell. Some are not as intense as mine and some may be much worse. In the end, this is information that is a part of defining who I am and how I survived. This is not particularly the type of information you discuss at work, trying to become an executive. When stories like this surface in some companies, you *could* be perceived as less than those other executives who have something to offer from their upbringing (i.e., information about good golfing or good private schools). You may believe your story will show how you beat the odds and prevail; however, it may also paint you with a boardroom brush that says, "not refined," "ghetto boy/girl," "not what we want." I personally felt ashamed of learning that my father was a drug dealer and was actually no more than a sperm donor as a dad. I kept this information from everyone who didn't need to know. If I had to do it all over again, I probably would have still kept this information out of the boardroom solely based on the atmosphere of the companies I previously worked. Today, I do feel my story shows how people can prevail and overcome any number of adversities and situations. However, if you are trying to get to the executive suite, tread cautiously when sharing this type of story with other executives. If your story is not the norm in your company when compared to the stories Buffy and Biff would share with the executive team, think twice before sharing yours. The executive area is not a fair and level playing field, and such information may not be a good thing to share.

Chapter 2

High School Is My Life

One of the key issues missed by many educators is the "serious" impact a stressed home life truly has on a student's academic abilities. I experienced this stress every day throughout high school, and in order to deal with the pressures, I learned how to lie to my friends about my father when necessary and just get through the day. High school defines many phases of our lives, and its importance is sadly understood by many black students too late in the journey. This chapter details the high-school journey and the importance of taking it seriously for the entire four years.

I was not the most popular person in the school, but I was known by pretty much everyone. Many people in my high school knew me from selling Italian ices as a youngster and my all-city, all-state track-and-field success. I was involved in a few high-school committees such as the Future Business Leaders of America (FBLA) for a while, but I needed to make money and was forced to change my after-school activities to profit-making opportunities. When I started high school, I had no master plan beyond the ninth grade, let alone college. I had no idea what was supposed to happen after high school other than working full-time. The process of transitioning from high school to the workplace was a mystery and of very little concern. What I did understand during my early years in high school was that I wasn't going to be a sports superstar, and all I had going for me was my brain. Working hard labor through previous summer jobs gave me enough knowledge to know I did not want to be a laborer, and I did not want to be poor. In summary, I needed to get out of Yonkers, New York!

I believe the biggest disillusion I experienced in high school was the realization that I had no idea what having a career versus having a job was all about. I was never introduced to anyone in a high-level professional career outside of my teachers and my doctors. I cannot remember anyone in my neighborhood that was an attorney, doctor, banker, or any other such profession. As with a number of black families in low-income areas, my mother (along with my father who was not active in my growing life) was not a member of anything beyond the neighborhood such as the National Association for the Advancement of Colored People (NAACP) and Urban League. Meaning, after a long day at work, we did not participate in much beyond community events, which included the annual neighborhood block party and maybe the PTA. In my mind, careers for black men were just labor-based crap jobs that people worked and complained about every day while drinking beer and whisky. This is most likely the primary reason many black kids in low-income areas have no focus toward college. If everyone around you is working in very small businesses, low-level city-government positions, and as laborers, there is no access to professional conversations or mentorship. I also can only assume that somewhere in my high-school system there was a bit of prejudice going around because somehow, most of the black students were very late in getting into the college swing whereas most of the white students were off and running with teacher support. If not for a diligent guidance counselor (Ms. Taylor), who was aware of my good grades and forced me to examine the specifics of the college route, my whole life could be different today. Even though my brother was in Howard University for almost two years, the information and processes used for him to get accepted into Howard did not turn on any light bulbs for me in terms of preparing for college based on an already-existing blueprint.

I forged on through the tenth grade with the goal of increasing my understanding of what happens after high school and how I needed to prepare. To jumpstart my learning process, I worked a number of little jobs to help me learn more about professional careers. For starters, by chance I replied to a posting on the bulletin board to become a high-school page for a U.S. congressman. Based on my grades and the recommendations from a couple of teachers, I was granted an internship. As a result of working in the congressional environment, I improved my speech and presentation dramatically. This was my first taste of how a perceived educated professional worked and how they were compensated. Through this experience, I also gained access to a mainframe computer (Univac 1140 and Univac 1108) as a part of the government national systems. This was my introduction to basic computer programming and getting some basic calculus and statistics training.

I acquired many little tidbits of information concerning business as a page working for the congressman. The first item was the relationship between the boss and the worker. For the first time I learned what it takes to get fired from a job, the balance sheet issues associated with bills and payroll, and the basic fact that everyone has a boss.

I believe the biggest enlightenment was that even though these people had what I considered to be excellent professional careers, they all complained about not making enough money. Each person in the office (except the congressman) talked about getting out of government and moving into the private sector. In my discussion with a brother (attorney) who was the office manager, he explained to me that government jobs have salary caps, and once you make a decision to work for the government, you have a fixed salary and no bonuses. He also explained to me that in the private sector, people make bonuses ranging from $10,000 to over a million. For the first time I had a reference between college graduates, salaries, government, and public (publicly traded) and private companies. Also to my surprise, there were a number of black people in the various government offices that were basically with jobs but still living a low income. Meaning, some of the people (high-school graduates and dropouts with new focus) in the office were very low on the government pay scale and barely getting by. When my internship ended with the congressman, I migrated down the street, adjacent to city hall, to work at the Yonkers public library system, which in a period of one year improved my knowledge of the English language and English literature. As a matter of fact, by working with the many attorneys and teachers who requested assistance, I learned an extensive amount about professional writing and the jurisprudence system. All of my side discussions with these professionals made it very clear why it was important to become a professional and earn a professional salary. However, I still was totally clueless concerning the actual steps to get into college and become successful. I continued working in the dark about planning for college. I continued with the school year working by day and hanging out on the block by night.

As my high-school experience neared the end, I began to realize how unexciting it was. Basically, I went to school, worked, and hung out with my friends. My last year outside of school was filled with odd tragedy and other sad moments. My main boys were Abdi, Gomes, JD, Kerry, Buster, Paul, Poochie (David), Walter, and JoJo. We all have been friends since the age of five or ten. As with many black male high-school students, I had my share of mindless activities and near misses with heading down the wrong path. On a number of nights, Poochie, JoJo and I would purchase a fifth of Old English and drink for the sake of getting drunk. We would always end up throwing up, but we kept doing it anyway. Right now, I have no idea where Poochie is. I understand he still lives in Yonkers along with all of his brothers and sisters. JoJo, I understand, had a rough life shortly after leaving high school (I'm not sure if he actually graduated). Sadly, days after high school, JoJo's oldest sister and her daughter were murdered. We soon drifted apart and have not seen each other for at least twenty-four years.

At Gorton high school, we always played basketball after school at Trevor Park or Lake Avenue. Somehow, whenever I went to play ball, my friend Walter was always there. One evening, I remember Walter coming by to play basketball and disappearing off into the sunset. Walter was one of those guys in the neighborhood who was very quiet, well-known, and always on the move. He was a nice guy but a little bit elusive. After finishing our basketball game, we all headed home. The next morning, Walter was dead. Something occurred during some type of robbery in a local convenience store, and that was it. Walter died from a single shotgun blast from the owner of the store. I believe the most profound feeling I had over this was Walter was my age and would never grow up to experience anything more. I was lost in the thought that someone I talked to just hours ago and almost every day in school died. It was a very lost feeling.

Just prior to graduation, I had one of my saddest moments in high school. It was approximately ten o'clock at night, and I had

just left my friend Gomes's house in my old '72 Cougar. While
pulling away, apparently Gomes was yelling and screaming for
me to come back. I never heard him or looked back because I
had the music blasting. I soon learned that immediately after
leaving his home, some type of shunt buried beneath the skin of
his father's arm had ruptured, and his father was bleeding and
dying on the kitchen floor. Gomes ran out to call me back to
help get his father to the hospital, but I never looked back in the
mirror. Gomes's dad died that night, and still today I wish I had
looked back in my rearview mirror. Here we are over twenty-
four years later, and I still always look back whenever I pull away
from any location.

Most of my time after school was filled with my friends and me
walking the neighborhood blocks for hours until the late evening.
My friends were rarely invited into my home. I was always in
fear some type of drug activity might be going on, and they
would find out my father was dealing drugs, or we would be
raided by the police or drug-dealer thug killers, and I did not
want my friends to be hurt or appear to be involved in any way.
Since a few of us had beat-up cars, we also spent a lot of time
driving to many of New York's boroughs, house parties, and clubs
we could get into. I am sure somewhere in my subconscious are
recollections of unique experiences with my high-school buddies,
but for the most part, most of my memories are consumed with
reminders of the after-midnight life I was dealing with concerning
my father. I remember I was visiting the home of a high-school
girlfriend, and I had just come out of her home on South
Broadway in Getty Square. When I exited the storefront
apartment building where she lived, I was stopped by flashing
lights while her parents watched, and I was placed into the backseat
of the police car and driven away. It was a very scary and
embarrassing moment. The police took me around the corner,

left me in the back of the car, and went to a payphone. Shortly after returning to the car, the two cops told me my father was looking for me, did I know that! My first thought was my father was in jail or worse, and he was trying to reach me; however, it turned out he was looking for me, and I needed to get my ass home. When they returned me to the front of my girlfriend's house, she and her parents were still standing there, wondering what my criminal detainment was all about. I made up some BS story and moved on. However, her father was an auxiliary policeman, and I am sure he asked around and probably figured out some of what was going on.

MY FEAR OF MIDNIGHT

When my brother and I were kids, midnight was always an interesting time. On regular occasions, we would be sleeping and hear the house door close. We lived in the second-floor apartment, and I could hear my father coming up the stairs. It was a distinctive one-second-per-step stomp that my brother and I came to know well. When he finally made it into the apartment, everyone else's needs were secondary. At 2 a.m., he acted as if it was three in the afternoon and made all sorts of noise, waking up everyone in the building. I remember when we were much younger; we got involved in my father's life as a ghetto musician. Meaning, he never took lessons, but he was a magnificent pianist. My brother and I, on the other hand, were accomplished drummers. Some nights at two in the morning, my father would open all the windows and crank up his organ to play jazz. We would sometimes play until five in the morning and go to school dead tired. Now that I look back at the experience, my father could have easily become a professional jazz pianist and been very successful.

Once we got older, midnight took on an entirely new meaning. On a number of evenings during my last months in high school, my life was filled with doing things for my father. I came to understand this was my brother's task until he was accepted into Howard University and moved away. It was now my burden.

Almost every night, I found myself spending the wee hours of the morning counting drug money and cutting cocaine with dextrose and lactose. Between 11 p.m. to 3 a.m., I felt I was living two lives. It was very odd. When we were doing the drug thing, a sense of total fear would come over me because my father would also tell these horrific stories about men he knew along the way who were shot up, stabbed, or killed in horrendous ways as a result of the drug trade. I believe as a result of living this life with my father at such a young age, I became very hard in my heart. I was much more serious and mature than my friends.

The night when I turned against my father occurred sometime in March 1980. At 11 p.m. on a Thursday, my father called my mother, instructing her to cook some food and for me to bring it to Harlem. He also told her to have me bring some cake (code for drugs) and a few stacks of cash. At the time, I did not understand the codes and honestly thought only food was in the bags. As a result of having a car, I would have to bring my father food. I always hated doing that because whenever I went to Harlem, I had to stay for an extra two hours or so sitting with my father in the back of some unfurnished, cold room, playing the organ and banging on the drums. On this particular night, my father called and instructed me to get his bag, which was filled with all of whatever it was he was selling. On this trip, he told me to fill a bucket and keep it in the car with a mixture of water, Clorox, and something else I can no longer remember.

My instructions were if I get stopped by the police, I was to pour all of the "stuff" into the bucket. While my mother spent much of her time trying to protect my brother and me from issues in the street, she had no protection for us from our father. I guess I could have directly pleaded to her to do something, but history with my father prohibited me from making that an option without putting my mother in harm's way. The reason I never brought my mother into the conversation is because I remember being about ten or eleven years old and watching my father beat down my mother. I remember watching my mother lying on the floor, mouth bleeding and gasping for air and water. We all stood around for about five very long seconds, and finally my father told us to go get her some water. My brother and I were in shock at what we had witnessed. We lost a lot of respect for my father at that moment but also gained a sense of fear, repugnance, and intimidation.

Once I packed my car with my father's drugs, bucket, food, and money, I was so scared. The distance between our apartment in Yonkers and Luke's (my father) Thrift Shop or his social club across the street was about twenty miles. I was particularly scared because I was eighteen with the face of a thirteen-year-old. I was always stopped by the cops wanting to see my license. I had to take Broadway in Yonkers to Dykman Street in the Bronx. I sometimes also took the Major Degan, which would dump me off near Eighth Avenue (now Fredrick Douglass Avenue) into Harlem. At around 12:30 a.m., while traveling on Dykman Street, flashing lights came up behind me. The cops hopped out of the car so fast there was no time to open the bags and pour the drugs into the bucket. I just froze. When the cop came around to the car, shining his flashlight, I had already placed the food tray atop the bucket as if the bucket were a table. The cop asked me where I was going so fast and why I was out so late. I told the cop my father was a night security guard in a building in downtown Harlem, and I was bringing him food. I opened the top of the food tray, and he could clearly see the mixture of greens, cornbread, chicken, and tea. He told me to move on and slow down. The cop pulled away, and I stayed at the spot, shaking and crying for a bit. I wanted to just turn around and go home. I continued on my trip and finally reached my father. When I got there, he was there with all these other guys who looked like they were just released from prison. He was mad that it took me so long, and I told him the cops stopped me. His comment was, "Well, you must have made out all right since you're not in jail," and he started laughing. He took the drugs and told me to set the food up on the table. All I could think about was my few months until graduation and getting away from all the crap.

As the year concluded, I tried many things to avoid having to do more chores for my father. I tried hanging out at friends' homes past midnight, but when I got home, my task was waiting. I continued to do what I had to do and just tried not to think about it anymore and kept my schoolwork at the A and B level to ensure I had a way out.

As a high-school student, I knew all of my teachers on a first-name basis, and I still keep in touch with some of my high-school teachers after twenty years. As a quick side note, a reference letter from one of my high-school teachers assisted me with impressing a previous employer during my early executive career days and helped me land a job with an annual salary of $65,000.

With all the side issues going on with my father and other basic pressures of making it through that time in my life, I can only hope my story impressed upon sons, daughters, students, and parents the importance of keeping focus on your goals in high school. Success in high school *will* shape the rest of most people's lives. I understand how the life of the poor black student is one of much strife and perseverance just to get through both the school process and then the many after-school life issues. It can be done! As easy as it is to sit, complain, blame others, and relieve yourself of the struggle you are in, don't fall prey and give up. Just remember life is full of challenges, and each conquered quest takes you to your next level of success.

I intimately practiced what I am preaching concerning high school. I attribute my focus in high school to much of my success today. I will admit not all aspects were perfect, but by the grace of God, I followed my own plan for success in high school, which helped me move to the next level. I can today unequivocally make the statement that "a poor performance in high school will surely make the rest of your life much more difficult" and most likely limit your success, depending on your definition of success.

CHAPTER 3

College: Be Prepared or Be Gone

College is just so much "everything"! I ran into so many roadblocks and frustrating situations in college that I felt like someone was trying to make me quit. My college experience was almost a complete disaster. It all began with the fire in my home when I was a senior at Gorton High School in Yonkers, New York. Because of the fire, my college applications were either burned in the mailbox or rerouted to who knows where. Because nobody in my family was keeping track of anything and we were all just trying to recover from the fire, I was not in sync with the college admissions deadlines and simply blew valuable time. Whatever the case, calling the University of Maryland to get such status information over the phone was absolutely impossible. One weekend, after my summer job concluded, I decided to drive to Maryland and visit the University of Maryland College Park to see if I was accepted and what I had to do next. I remember going to the admissions office and feeling lost and intimidated beyond belief. I was by myself and in an environment full of guidelines, regulations, and procedures I did not know, and felt completely lost. I finally hooked up with a more sympathetic teacher's assistant in the waiting room and obtained the information I needed to find out at least what was going on. In short, the entire ordeal took hours just to determine if I was accepted at the university. Luckily, I had a driver's license because without one I would not have been able to pick up any of my personal application information. Sitting on a wall with an aching back, I read the material and was elated to find I had been accepted; however, I missed all the deadlines and was about to totally blow my opportunity to attend. I immediately launched a desperate plan to complete all my admissions requirements for entering the fall 1980 semester.

During the ordeal, I had no time to make a phone call to my mother, but when I did, I explained that school was starting in three days, and I did not know what to do. Because of my late replies to the university, I was not given a dorm-room assignment. I was told I would have to try again next semester for a dorm-room-and-board assignment.

Realizing I was on my own until next semester for housing and board, I hatched a plan to return quickly to New York, pack my clothes, and drive back to Maryland to stay with my uncle. The plan was to drive the University of Maryland crazy until they realized I was out of state and "required" a room assignment or I would be out on the street. The plan did not work out at all. When I returned to Maryland, I ended up staying with my high-school friend Abdi at Howard University in DC for a couple of weeks. The overall surprise of going to college left me without notebooks, pens, or pencils during my first day of classes. To get by, I borrowed a pen from a student and wrote my notes on napkins. This went on for about four days or so. On a couple of nights, I actually slept in my car in the parking lot at the University of Maryland because of a few early classes. I would have stayed with my brother at Howard, but he was being moved around by the housing department and was hard to reach. Each day I drove up Rhode Island Avenue from Howard University to the University of Maryland to attend classes. Eventually, my constant nagging at the university housing department paid off. I was given a room assignment after about a month and met my college roommate (of four years), Ollen.

My first night in the college dorm was like a new world. Finally, I was not begging someone to let me up in a Howard dorm, sleeping in my car, or trying to sneak into the cafeterias at Howard or Maryland to get food. I was so relieved and tired. I finally took the time to get proper notepads and unpack my clothes. After a few nights together, Ollen and I realized we had something in common. We both loved music. He had a plethora of music equipment and records, and so did I. Before we knew it, we blended the two systems together and added a mixer to mix records. One night, during an ad hoc mixing session, we ran into our first hall party filled with drunken students and naked white women running through our room. It was so wild. Over time, we simply got used to the campus happenings and just went on with our day. We eventually formed Wood-O Productions, which made us very popular on campus. We were one of a few black DJs on campus, hosting most of the parties for black students and black organizations. It was great! I had a hard time making my way though college, but it did help to have a few friends along the way (especially in a big ten predominantly white university). As expected, most of the activities throughout the college were geared toward white students. In a push to make some changes, a friend, Charles, and I petitioned the student council about the low level of diversity within the student community. After much lobbying, we were allotted funds, and we created a new organization called Together for a Change (TFC). This was a short-lived, two-year organization; however, during the time we were in operation, we hosted a few student-awareness sessions, volleyball parties, and dorm parties. I felt good doing something different for every black student in such a barely diverse environment.

Financing college was very difficult. I was always in a constant search for tuition funding and money to avoid being broke all the time. I remember applying for financial assistance with the United Negro College Fund (UNCF) and being turned down. I thought that was interesting since my mom was listed as a single parent and barely had any money, making only $15,000 annually with two kids in college. I guess there is always someone poorer out there looking for college cash.

To get through college, I worked two jobs. During the day, I worked about six hours a day between classes at the educational technology department, and at night, during the graveyard shift, I worked five hours at a DC-based national cable television station. I typically slept only three to five hours a night for three years in college. Whatever my part-time TV job did not cover for my college costs, Pell Grants were used to get me through along with guaranteed student loans. Most of my on-campus work went to paying off my college bill or college credits for work to boost my GPA. If you attend a predominantly white school, don't look for anyone to reach out to you as a black student. You need to do the reaching out to cope with all the issues you face. I remember being a sophomore and trying to apply for an internship. In order to do so, I needed the endorsement of one of my professors. When I asked my professor for his signature, I was told he would not sign off because I was only a first-semester sophomore. The next day, I was having a conversation with him in his office, and to my surprise, a friend (a Biff) came in with the same class ranking as I and obtained my professor's signature and permission. I discussed the issue with Biff after class and waited for him to start his internship. I then went to the professor with my proof of inconsistency and obtained the approval I needed. In college you need to recognize you are no longer a high-school student (although you may still feel like one during the early years), and you need to take care of all your business. If you are being treated wrong, go after making it right. Do not run from necessary confrontation and get what is owed to you as a paying student. I dealt with many tiny racist issues at Maryland, but I made it through the process.

During my entire college experience, I dealt with many things. In addition to dealing with the murder of my father, I also broke my shoulder in gymnastics, witnessed college students being turned into prostitutes, and watched a number of college students leave the university due to breakdowns over the pressures of college life. I personally witnessed at least four students being hit by cars because they were too drunk, as well as, watched the police deal with the results of a young college student who took a suicide dive out of her dorm room window. The saddest memory I have about college was that of a well-known basketball player in my senior year doing well during the NBA draft and obtaining a multimillion-dollar contract. After leaving the NBA draft, he returned to Maryland and died after trying hard drugs for the first time. He had attended a number of parties Ollen and I had thrown over the years and lost it all over trying drugs during the happiest moment of his life.

In my junior year, I was almost kicked out of Maryland because I ran out of money. Chase Manhattan Bank sent my check to the house in Jamaica Queens Since I was still a resident of New York. When I left for college, my mother had decided to move back to Charleston, South Carolina, after my father's death. My brother was living in the old house in Queens. I called New York and asked my brother if my student-loan check arrived. He told me it arrived, and I immediately drove home to get it since time was running out. When I arrived in New York, my brother could not find my check. We looked for hours around the house, and it was nowhere to be found. That single issue launched a ton of quagmires for me in the area of university politics and forced me to miss two weeks of classes since my bill was not paid. Since the funds were committed, the school allowed me to stay and eat, but it was very difficult for me to catch up. My brother and I did not talk for a while after that; however, we had been through a lot together as brothers and best friends, so it wasn't long before I was calling him in New York or he was calling me. I was totally on my own in college. During my entire four years, I believe my mother visited the campus once, and my brother and uncle, a few times as well. I heard from my friends by phone a few times, and that was it. I basically stayed at the University of Maryland the entire time including summers for summer school and working both jobs.

At graduation, my grades were pretty good, but all the constant work and other issues made it very difficult to be an A student. I graduated as a mostly B-plus and C student overall; however, all the hands-on work in technology (satellite and computers) as a student for three years left me with extensive experience far beyond the average college student. By the time I graduated, I knew most of my professors personally. I was also senior technician in the technology center at Maryland and managed the overnight (graveyard shift) crew at the cable television station. During my last semester, I ran out of money and had to get off the university meal plan. I found myself with a dorm room and no money in my pocket. All of the money I was making "had to" go into the bank for an apartment after graduation. Each meal I paid for put the chance of getting the apartment in jeopardy and possibly forcing me to move back to New York or South Carolina after graduation. I called on friends to sneak food for me out of the dining hall, and thank God for good friends. I also put a hot plate in my room and cooked nauseating but cheap food many nights to get through. On a number of nights, I simply went to bed very hungry and ate whatever was free when I arrived at the TV station at midnight and in the morning for the breakfast crew.

After graduation, I was set and ready to get on with life, having two jobs lined up for postgraduation. Not all things were perfect, but I reached my goals. The starvation of my last semester left me with an overall weight of 125 pounds. I was tired all the time. I remember nothing about my graduation day. After it was all over, in reflection, I realized I missed out on many of the services the University of Maryland had to offer me as a student. After graduation, I ran into a number of white alumni who told me of free golf lessons, bowling parties in the on-campus bowling alley, and many other such events. All of these events I missed out due to all the work and the fact that many black students knew nothing of such services.

After my college experience, I realized how important it is to share our stories of how we made it through as black people. Sharing information about our lives as black college students will only help others learn how to get by regardless of the adversities we face. So many black students land in college environments and know nothing about its operations, how to deal with issues, and simply how to survive. This still happens today. We can all do a better job. If you are a black student or a parent of a black student going to college or already in college, it is important that everyone understands how different the environment influences students. When possible, if only by phone, keep in contact regularly as parent/guardian and young-adult student. Only fifty percent of the typical college students' day is dedicated to school. The rest of the time is "something else." Know what that something else is as a parent because many times it could change the course of your kid's life. When I completed my college experience, I reaffirmed my commitment to continue documenting my journey in order to offer insight to others later in life. While high school was the most impressive, college was the most critical and pressurized situation, affecting me emotionally, physically, and financially. This is not a time to separate as parent and young adult.

CHAPTER 4

The Postgraduate Awakening

After graduating from college, one year begins to blend into the next without differentiation, and before you know it, some type of career formed, and you have to examine where you are to see if you stayed on track.

When I left the calm domicile of my dorm room at the University of Maryland, my graveyard-shift job at a local cable television station was in full swing, and I was good to go for postgraduation. I also hung on to my on-campus job for some extra money for six hours during the day. As planned, I leased my first apartment in Riverdale, Maryland, and kept my car tuned and running. Approximately thirty minutes after graduation, the cold, hard facts of the real world hit me in the face. When I returned to my apartment after the graduation ceremony, I found my apartment had been ransacked and burglarized. A box of six-hundred-plus pictures documenting my college life had been stolen along with my Pentax camera with telephoto lens. While I missed the camera, losing the pictures was distressing since I was documenting my journey. This was my reminder and warning that I was no longer in the bosom of a protected college campus and I needed to be more careful.

Shortly after getting settled into my new postgraduation lifestyle, I realized my graveyard-shift cable television job wasn't exactly paying me enough money to live comfortably on my own. I knew the better salaries could only be achieved by moving to the day shift and meeting more people. While I was one of the best engineers in Master Control engineers, setting up satellite feeds, directing call-in shows, running audio, and managing the studio, my multiple request to move to the day shift fell on deaf ears. What also became apparent to me was the graveyard shift was the "training" ground for new tech staff. Over a period of months, I noticed new white recruits trained by me during the graveyard shift were being given opportunities to move off the graveyard shift and over field work or the day-shift studio positions. Again, I requested a change for myself. No change. At that point, I began trying to figure out what else I could do. I decided to put my interest in finance, and I began working in a local Silver Spring, Maryland, branch of a New York-based investment company while still holding down my graveyard-shift job. The problem with keeping both jobs was that in order for me to become a stock / mutual fund broker, I had to study extensively during the day, and the overall amount of study made it impossible for me to get enough sleep to handle the graveyard shift. For a few months, I was a walking zombie. Because of the fatigue, my studying was lackluster and my master control work was lackluster. I had to make a decision. Since most of the people in the investment office were living nicely and most of the people in the backroom of the television study were living paycheck-to-paycheck lives, I quit my cable TV job, assuming the grass was greener on the other side.

Shortly after obtaining my securities licenses, I realized the leads given to me by the office investment manager were dead leads that had been called before by other brokers. I was told that if I did not like the sales leads, I was given to go to the "U.S. Broker Sales Generation Organization," which was an office joke for "pull out the phone book and start cold-calling some folk.

I later learned that those "posh-living" brokers in the office (Biffs and Buffys) had wealthy parents and friends who were buds with the company office manager. In short, they were given the quality sales leads while people like me was given sales leads filled out by people who thought they were signing up for a contest or a free vacation trip. After a few months of my new 100-percent-commission job, I was almost totally broke. I had to either push hard, close some deals, or move on to a new job.

One night, my white manager accompanied me on a third house visit with a black family in DC who had a bit of cash as thirty-five-year veteran teachers. The woman's name was Mrs. McCloud, and she had all of her money in a tax sheltered annuity (TSA), which is common for teachers, and she planned on pulling from the fund for retirement in five years. My manager suggested a plan for her to roll her funds into a front-loaded mutual fund (a plan that takes almost 30 percent up-front day one of what you put into the fund for management fees) and some five-year bonds. As a broker, I would have received an excellent commission; however, for Mrs. McCloud and her family, it would have been a disastrous mistake. When we left the client's house that night, I questioned my manager about the financial plan he suggested, and his comment was, "She got hers, and now it's mine." I put off my next meeting with Mrs. McCloud for two weeks, and my manager finally forced me to close. I remember the long drive to her home (with my car riding on vapors and only $25 left to my name), and coming to the conclusion, I could not trick this nice black woman into this plan. When I arrived at her home, I left the paperwork in my car. When I entered her home, she was so excited to be doing something with her money. As a matter of fact, in her mind, this move might allow her to retire earlier than five years. When I sat down at her kitchen table, I told her what had occurred and that I thought she should leave

her money where it was. I offered a safer solution, directing her
to a different company. To my surprise, she had been talking to
another broker (white), and they too were suggesting something
just as radical. To ease her nerves, I suggested she call her union
reps to confirm my new plan. As I left her home, she stopped me
at the door and asked, "What will happen to you over this?" I
told her I will be out of a job and will have to figure out what to
do from here. She asked if I was financially OK (I was
underweight and dressing well), and I said not really, but I will
be OK. She offered me $100 for helping her, but I refused. The
next day, Mrs. McCloud called me at my apartment and told me
her union reps at AFSME told her I was totally correct and her
loss would have been devastating. Ready to resign, I packed up
and drove to the brokerage office. When I arrived, it was about
4:30 p.m. I checked in and went to the back where the training
room was to return some manuals. While in the back, I heard
the manager and a few Biffs come into the office, and in their
discussions, my manager talked about how he gave me moldy
leads. I also heard someone say that even if I had done well on
my own, "a nigger would never run this office." I'm not sure if it
was the manager or the white broker who made the comment,
but both seemed comfortable enough to chuckle afterward. He
was a native Bostonian. I came out of the back of the office,
looked at him, and simply said, "I guess I need to switch to
another office now that I know the rules here." This was my first
hard-hitting introduction to racism. It hurt, but it did not seem
to sting because I also realized I did not like sales, so I felt I
would never face this again.

After my goal of becoming rich as a stockbroker was squashed to
hell, I was starving Marvin. I had change for gas money, bread
for food, and an apartment I was barely paying for and behind
on my rent. To survive I called a temp agency and spent the next

four months working in a paint factory and lumberyard and moving furniture. I was always tired and forced to file for hardship to delay paying back my student loans. This was my lowest moment. I felt like a total failure concerning my personal goals. I was a college graduate working next to people who dropped out of high school, lived in trailers, and had rotten teeth. My heart and spirits were broken. One day, while I was sitting in my empty apartment, I remember how my father turned his life around in a blink of an eye. I called some old contacts and put the drug trade (as a courier or something) on the table as a serious possibility. When I realized despair had gotten the best of me, I dropped the idea, called off my contacts, and sat alone for a week, trying to figure out how to correct my situation. I remember just barely paying my rent and having absolutely no money. For the first time in my life, I had no money for anything. I turned to a pouch I had been carrying around with me for over twelve years. It was full of mint condition antique coins I'd been collecting most of my life. I sold most of my most valuable coins for another three months of survival—for the rent, gas, and insurance. I needed each to be able to continue moving on. Before long, I was totally broke again. My car was out of gas so I had to take the bus or walk. In the dead of winter in Maryland, I walked three miles to a small convenience store with only enough money to get a newspaper and continue hunting for a job. I found about six jobs in the newspaper to apply for, but I estimated that by the time any employer tried to call me back, my phone would be turned off for nonpayment. Also, if I was lucky to secure a job, my first pay check would come too late to avoid an eviction. It was time to take a step backward in order to move forward. I decided to sublet my apartment to a relative, and I stayed in my uncle's home in Oxon Hill rent free for a while. I cashed in more old coins and held on to the $500 from the sale for as long as I could. In no time, I found a new job as a fiber-optical technician

THE GLASS IN MY THROAT

in a high-tech company. My spirits were high, and I was finally in an improved office setting, something I felt I deserved as a college graduate. The only problem with the job was I lived in Oxon Hill, Maryland, and the job was in Reston, Virginia (fifty-mile driving distance). The $300 was enough to get me there for two weeks and collect my first paycheck. On my first day of the job, I was told by the owner that the company lost the contract it was awarded, but they would honor my position (and that of a few others) at the rate of $4 per hour. I was so tired I had no choice but to accept the offer. With such a low salary, it only took a short while for the driving to eat up all my cash and for my car to deteriorate. I had limited health insurance and was not allowed to take a day off for Christmas (Jewish owner); my car insurance went up because of the distance I was driving, and my student-loan payment was headed for default. Time for another change!

While I was still poor and struggling, I did have a few dollars and learned a lot about fiber-optic technology. I spent cash on every local newspaper I could find and talked to everyone about a new job. I remember reading about a nonprofit organization e-mail systems manager position. I was no e-mail expert, but I knew just as much as the next guy. I remember standing in the technology lab of the optical company and getting the call that the e-mail job was mine. The entire room seemed brighter, and all I needed was the offer letter in my hand. Later that day, the offer letter was faxed to the fax machine of the optical company, and I gave my notice. Soon after, I was in my new job as a computer tech making $25,000 a year. Life never seemed so great. The only problem was that my car died, and I was relying on public transportation. At first I was upset and not used to conforming to someone else's schedule, but I got with the program. I rode public transportation for almost two years.

While at this nonprofit organization, I began working on and improving existing processes and submitting some of my own ideas in software development. After creating a few prototypes, I approached my manager with a concept to use the e-mail system as a vehicle for delivering mortgage-related application data. He thought it was a good idea. Within weeks, I visited a friend at the Department of Housing and Urban Development and demonstrated my idea. Within a few weeks, my program was piloted within the HUD agency and was eventually rolled out to many mortgage companies around the United States. The application generated much revenue for the organization and nearly because an industry standard. I continued to develop applications, and eventually more programmers were hired. I was moved to the position of vice president and given a big private office in Washington DC. I soon learned that managers (Biffs and Buffys) who were hired to run other aspects of the new company (funded by my application development) were making more than $120,000 a year in salary alone. After learning this, I asked for an increase to $35,000 (naive). To my surprise, the answer was no. In disbelief, I began looking for a new job. I soon left the nonprofit company after accepting a position with a local savings bank.

My move to the savings bank, at the time, appeared to be one of the best decisions of my life. When I arrived at the savings bank, I was welcomed and given a nice manager's cubicle. I was responsible for local area networks, desktops, and software installation. Two weeks after being in my new position, a new Buffy was appointed the head of my division. She knew nothing about technology, and shortly after taking the helm, she brought in a friend of hers who had the same limited knowledge qualifications. Late one evening, while they thought they were alone, a colleague (white female) and I were in the server area and heard the two discussing how they wanted to have an "all girls" department. Over a period of eight months, my boss treated me like crap. She micromanaged me to the minute and told me I was lucky to have a job. In the eight months I was at the bank, I installed new legal systems, phone-banking systems, imaging systems, Wang system updates, and much more. I was known all over the bank by all managers. It became a situation where other managers would not meet with my manager or her other hired guns unless I was at the meeting. They felt she did not have the technical knowledge and I needed to be present to explain the details. At the end of my first year of employment, the CEO decided to examine new technology and wanted to hire or promote someone to the position of director of new technology. Unfortunately for me, my manager controlled the information on the position numbers and refused to communicate the information to me because she didn't want me to apply. For two weeks I was told she had not posted the position. Luckily for me, my girlfriend (my wife now of thirteen years) worked in human resources. I obtained the job posting-number from her and submitted my application. When my manager found out I submitted my application (knowing I was in good with the CEO), a chain of events occurred. Two days after submitting my application, I called HR for confirmation and status and was told my application was not received. I contacted the vice president of HR and was given consistent misleading information. Finally, my girlfriend checked and found they had received my resume and was purposely doing nothing to include me in the review. They were stonewalling me until I missed the submission date. While I don't remember the exact details, my girlfriend somehow set up an interview for me with HR. Knowing who I was and colluding with my manager, the HR manager suggested I did not have the experience without actually reading my resume. I explained who I was and gave more than twenty internal contacts including the CEO and chief corporate counsel as references. While going through this web of HR subterfuge, the position was given to another person selected by my manager. My girlfriend was devastated! She observed the injustice from inside the department and saw how favoritism and racism worked as a machine from the inside. She later said to me if she had not seen it for herself, she would have assumed I was telling a big tale.

After my ordeal with HR, a week later, I received a call from my old employer (the nonprofit company). Apparently, they did not know how to build on my ideas for software development and wanted me back. Sales were flat or dying, and the software had no feature updates since my departure. After my experience with the savings bank, I returned to the nonprofit organization. My return sparked interest with customers, and I began developing new ideas and concepts onto the software platform and creating totally new business opportunities. On a trip to a friend's wedding midweek, I remember being on the Amtrak train to New York. The first call I received on my portable phone pack told me I had been moved by the CEO to the business development group. Thirty minutes later, I received a call telling me the whole business development group was being let go and the company was being sold. It appeared the goal was to sell the company from the very beginning of my return. Selling the company was difficult because the company software had become stale and sales were flat. The CEO's idea was to bring back the creator of the software (me) to spark new interest with customers on the up tick and sell the company. My infusion of life back into the development process showed enough signs of life for the company to be sold. Just prior to being laid off, my girlfriend and I got married and bought a new townhouse in Upper Marlboro, Maryland. What a way to start a new marriage. During my downtime, I recouped and tried to leave all the personal baggage of unfair play in the workplace behind me; however, the last hit on my career cost me a corporate-ladder level, forcing me to take a step backward.

I soon found a new job and spent the next two years in the Washington, DC area. I steadily moved up the low-level management ranks, making my way to being a legitimate assistant vice president in Fortune 1000 companies. I eventually left DC and moved on to Philadelphia where creating my mold for the executive ranks truly began.

I am sure many other black men and women have similar stories. Somehow the experiences get thrown into the pot of simply "paying your dues." I disagree with any suggestion that what I went through was me "fairly" paying my dues. I found my experience gave me a view behind the scenes concerning the extra advantages given to too many Biffs and Buffys to make climbing the corporate ladder much easier. On many occasions, I have had a number of Buffys (and a couple of Biffs) tell me they don't understand why they were being promoted or given certain opportunities when I had been there longer or had more background and understanding. I will not say all Biffs and Buffys experience this push or that all companies exercise unfair employment practices at the management levels. The fact of the matter is I experienced such treatment regularly going after the big-fish jobs. I am sure other qualified blacks have also come up against this unfair pseudofriendship, racist, and nepotistic perpetual support system designed to a prestine work environment. Such favoritism is why affirmative action was put into place in the first place.

CHAPTER 5

Building the Executive Mold

Everything you do in your career becomes a building block to creating your personal executive mold. What is particularly important is "your ability to manage." It is imperative that you focus on a path and on events that will make you someone's supervisor or boss. The bottom line in being an executive is all about managing people, setting directions, and making decisions. Until you move to the forefront of being a part of the management decision-making process, you will not be on the path to becoming a true executive. This basic principle is the same as if you are trying to become a high-level executive in an existing company or trying to launch a new company yourself as an entrepreneur. You can be a cog in the corporation completing many successful projects, but none of those types of successes will move you on to the executive management track. Before I graduated from college, I was managing a staff of eight student workers at the campus technology center, and during the overnight shift at the television station, I was managing college students and employees as the senior master-control person. Working in a supervisory capacity gave me the ability to plan everyone's activities for the day and learn how to gain the trust of my superiors concerning my ability to set and execute plans.

During the periods I hit hard times and found myself working in a paint factory and lumberyard, I quickly moved up the ladder

THE GLASS IN MY THROAT 57

(in a matter of weeks) to becoming a supervisor. Becoming a supervisor will be your introduction to dealing with people and their problems (and issues) on a daily basis. You will begin to deal with the many creative excuses employees can come up with concerning tardiness, sickness, theft, and other employee-relations issues. You will deal with the personal fear that sometimes comes with the hostility of a fired employee. You will learn how to deal with the financial impact to employees when you must inform them that Christmas bonuses are much less than expected. Do not kid yourself; if your goal is to make it to the executive suite, your day will be filled with communicating good, bad, and devastating news to employees. This level of management is not always easy or personally rewarding.

In addition to learning to deal with employees, you must also dispose of your "awe" when in the presence of top executive personnel. Typically, when the CEO, president, or other chief staff members of a company walks into a room, a level of awe and intimidation comes into play. People become somewhat starstruck and forget their main points, as well as their willingness to speak up. As a part of building your executive mold, you will have to learn how not to lose your edge and focus when such personnel is in your presence. You must learn how to communicate good and bad news to both the masses and other senior executive personnel. You must become accustomed to direct confrontation as the norm versus the odd situation. I remember working as a vice president in a large financial institution and walking into a room of mainframe programmers who felt a certain new technology was risky for the bank to utilize as a primary technology platform. It was my first week at the bank, and I was asked to confirm or reject the position of the mainframe programmers and systems group. As a new technology person who understood the new technology in detail, I had no choice but to reject the mainframe group's position in a public setting.

During the meeting, I faced much scrutiny and made no friends. While this situation was a disaster for me at the lower-management level, it was a total success for me at the executive ranks. In the end, I was correct with my assumptions concerning new technology, and those who were watching from the executive perch made it possible for me to move from a vice president to a senior vice president in only a year.

As much as I would love to say all things are equal in business, I cannot. In many ways, I found that I faced issues other managers (Biffs) did not face, and not having a host of friends and colleagues who were also black and already in the executive ranks made it more difficult for me to determine if I was being treated fairly financially and personally. I had no blueprint to work from.

In my early thirties, I landed on a job with a very large regional bank in Philadelphia. I was recognized as a leader in the technology field and given the opportunity to do many things as an assistant vice president. Since I was a first-line executive, the bank bought my house in Maryland and relocated my wife and me to the Philly region. I was given something within $50,000 as a signing bonus and a temporary setup in corporate housing for migrating executives (with maid service) until we found a new home in the area.

Within the first year of being at the bank, I spearheaded the installation of check-imaging systems, communications systems, and other much-needed solutions. The primary focus was to assist the bank in starting a new subsidiary in the third-party processing arena. After having a successful run in the third-party side of the company, I moved over in 1995 to the formal (consumer-based) bank. When I made this move, I learned *humongous* lessons. In my move over to the formal bank, I was promoted to the level of a full vice president for all my prior successful work. During my induction, I noticed that I was on the lowest rung of vice presidentship. The level I was given was just one point shy of receiving the "real benefits" as an executive. I disputed the issue for a month or so and was assured the ranks at the level I was demanding were full. All incoming vice presidents in IT would be at the same entry level. Two months later, a new Buffy came with a vice-president level and the large benefits I was denied. As the excuses flew, I realized I reached the next level of racism. The funny thing about racism is that it always looks different than the last experience you survived. You don't always see it coming, but when it shows itself, you recognize it immediately.

Since my goal was to reach the executive level of "chief" (i.e., chief information officer, chief technology officer, chief operating officer), I had to recognize I did make a giant step to the VP level in one and a half years where others waited much longer. I was a seriously aggressive black man with a boyish face that would fool many people. I understood corporate politics and played the game very well (if I should say so myself). As I examined my new surroundings as a vice president, I realized one big change. Most of my job was about managing, and not doing. As a technology person, that is a tough road to cross. I was a heavy detail-oriented person in all areas of applications development, network design, project management, imaging, and much more. I realized how the shop manager felt when they became the foreman and no longer worked shoulder to shoulder with the crew. This was a massive change. I also learned that the art of written communication was seriously different. My communication skills changed from communicating the how to communicating why, how much, and how long.

As an executive manager, I needed to learn much more than my craft. I needed to become more intimate with the company business, financials, and strategy. I quickly determined that learning more about accounting (i.e., left and right side of the balance sheet) since accounting would be primary to understanding the company's bottom line which is professionally known as EBITDA (earning before interest, taxes, depreciation, and amortization),. Before my new mold was complete, I had to meet the beast one more time.

When I moved over to the bank, I created a very diverse team of blacks, Asians, and whites. It was the most diverse area in information technology. My team supported me, and I supported them. However, the work I was involved with was met with much jealously by other white men who had been with the bank much longer and were upset they were not given my position. By the end of my first year as a senior vice president, I was responsible for electronic data interchange (EDI), enterprise document imaging, and moving the bank to a new customer technology called the Internet and away from closed online systems such as Prodigy and CompuServe. One afternoon, during a conference call, four Biffs from another IT support group called my assistant vice president (a black woman) a "black gorilla monkey skank" during the phone conversation. We also later learned the same group of men was using secret mainframe program passageways to corrupt our programs. Before I knew it, it was an all-out race war in the bank between my group and some of the Biffs who wanted my position from the very beginning. Things really escalated when an Asian woman on my team received a pseudo-death threat to give to my black female AVP. Before I knew it, we had guards walking my team to their cars in the evening. I soon tired of the entire atmosphere and simply quit. My anger over quitting my job over such an issue was appalling. I received a number of calls from top bank executives, asking me to stay with the bank, and after some serious convincing, I decided to stay; however, I was still actively looking for a new job. The overall event set me up for the next phase as an executive in corporate America.

The final component to building your executive mold is to deal with the feelings of taking risks. This is a very tricky feeling to deal with. Can you imagine a young black executive living on a $75,000-plus salary with a good bonus situation having to make the decision to leave what he or she has built for something else that may or may not work out? It takes so much for black people to reach such ranks; taking such risk seems almost suicidal. While making this decision is tremendously difficult, it is a standard component of the typical executive ordeal. At one point in my career, my wife and I had to weigh the risk of me taking a $50,000 cut from my base salary for a better overall compensation package across the board. However, if the opportunity did not work out, we would have had to deal with a possible $150,000 total loss annually. Risk is very much a part of the executive picture and more so for the black executive since we typically do not have rich relatives and friends to help us pick up the pieces financially by lending us $50,000 here and there. Remember, there are only a few top-level executive positions available at any given point in time, and when most of these jobs are filled, for whatever reason, there is a very low percentage filled by blacks or other minorities. Hence, making a decision to walk away from a profitable executive position for another is a pretty serious situation.

CHAPTER 6

Beware of the Interview Intake Process

Looking for a new job at the executive level was totally new to me. In the beginning, I searched various newspapers such as the *Wall Street Journal Employment Weekly* and the *Philadelphia Inquirer*, looking for jobs. Whatever the case, it took months! While I was going through this process and still working for the bank, news was released that the bank was cutting jobs and possibly up for sale. The pressure was on; I needed to find a new job quickly.

One of the most unbelievable experiences I had while looking for a job during this time was the speed at which I would get a call back from employers after they received my resume via fax or e-mail. On many occasions, employers would almost offer me the job prior to the interview. My telephone presence exhibited no Ebonics, and my voice is very deep, like that of a radio personality. In most cases, the person on the other side assumed I was a six foot two inch white male with blond hair, blue eyes, and a killer resume. I was the perfect candidate over the phone.

It was at this point that I ran into a new tool used in the racist repertoire of unfair hiring practices. Before I was allowed to meet with possible employers, I was asked to have a preliminary "videoconference" meeting. From the very moment videoconferencing came into play, I felt it was not going to help my situation at all. I remember one particular videoconference call where I purposely arrived late, leaving enough time for the team on the other side to fully assemble, instead of not showing up (hiding out of the view of the camera) once they saw that I was black. What made this particular videoconference meeting so special was that it was my second interview after the one that was held by voice-conference call. During the voice conference-call, I went toe-to-toe with all their top technology people, and they basically offered me the job on the phone. They even went as far as to FedEx me health forms and employee handbook and give me information about a corporate picnic about to take place in a week, which I would attend even though my possible starting date would be after the picnic date.

When I arrived late, I could see five employees on the other side (two white women and three white men including the company CFO and COO). When I sat down, I could basically see them go stoned-faced, and the CFO and COO looked at each other and slumped down in their chairs. Fifteen minutes into the call, all the officers had to step out for an emergency, leaving only the HR person. I was never called back, and even the recruiter was surprised by what occurred. This loop of surprise with white executives occurred multiple times. I traveled to places like Pittsburg, Atlanta, and Miami, and each time, all was well on the phone, but when I returned home, I never heard from either the company or the executive recruiters. In one situation, a comment was made to the recruiter such that my recruiter called me and told me the president is a prejudiced person and we need to start looking at another company.

Another insulting situation was when I applied for the executive vice president / chief information officer position at a successful financial dot-com. By the time I resigned from the bank, I had reached the corporate level of senior vice president and crossed the six-digit money meter. During the interview at this dot-com, I was given a technical architecture document by their top tech person who would be working for me if I was selected. The goal was for me to explain what was going on in this document, which they paid a technology-consulting company to create. During the interview, I highlighted flaws in the architecture and identified a number of issues. To my surprise, one of the people in the audience was from the consulting company. He confessed they did not take the issues I raised into consideration, and they would go back and redesign. When the representative from the consulting company left, I told them I was being nice and there were more issues in the mix that still needed to be addressed (I held back some information until I got the job). After sitting for almost forty-five minutes, waiting for someone to return to the room, the HR person came to me, suggesting I need to take a test. I was looking at the agenda, and there was nothing on the agenda about taking an exam. Also, as a top executive, I found this very surprising. Since I needed the job, I submitted to the test. The test was basically at the level of a civil service exam, asking me to calculate basic math and alphabetize lists. Halfway through the test, the CEO and HR person returned, and I asked why I was taking the test. They told me all candidates have to go through the test. I told them I have tons of experience, demonstrated my experience with their tech consulting firm, have excellent references at the executive level they could call, and have a college degree from the University of Maryland. After the conversation, I called the recruiter using the phone in the conference room where I was taking the test and told him about what was going on. He called the chief operating officer, and I could hear a bit of a riff on the phone. I realized they simply wanted me out (I saw no blacks during my site tour) and stopped taking the test and walked out.

I was very distraught by what I was going through and realized it would be excruciatingly difficult getting selected at this new level. I thought about saving myself the headaches and including Kappa Alpha Psi (black fraternity) or my picture on my resume to get the issue out of the way and meet only with companies willing to actually "practice" executive-level diversity rather than simply publicize diversity for the purpose of feeling good about themselves and appeasing clients. I was afraid I would kill being able to get my foot in the door and continued down the same path of not highlighting that I was black on my resume. Perseverance and confidence did eventually overshadow most of these issues, and eventually some doors began to open.

After five months, I had a few offers under consideration when I received a call that would change the entire course of my career and bring me to the ultimate executive level I'd been seeking, which was becoming a *chief information technology officer.*

CHAPTER 7

Going Off on My Own (or sort of)

In 1996, I spent months playing games with potential employers who loved my background but did not want me representing their company at the top executive level for information technology. I wanted to believe there was another reason companies would turn cold toward me, but conversations with a few recruiters after the fact confirmed the elusiveness of diversity at the executive ranks.

In June of 1996, I received a call from a friend (we'll call him Mr. D), who worked at the regional bank I was still working at in Philadelphia. The bank was on a cost-cutting path, and he and another gentleman Mr. F opted out of the bank for a nice severance package. Mr. D told me he was working on an idea and wanted to give me a call later to discuss a unique opportunity. Two months later, I was still looking for a new job, and Mr. D's business plan was sounding pretty good to start a financial processing company. In his search for funding, Mr. D had reached a point where they needed my help. In a nutshell, they formulated a financial plan and strategy for the business and had shopped it around on Wall Street. Wall Street was lackluster on the plan because it was missing a sound technology strategy. Their request was for me to develop the technology plan, and if funding was obtained, they would bring me on board. Having been burned by a number of white business owners during my recent experience with the hiring process, I was very nervous about Mr. D. keeping his word and not just stealing my technology plan and then hiring a Biff. I told my wife I could easily create the plan, but I was concerned that I would simply be used. In the end, I decided to "trust" Mr. D and Mr. F and create a plan that would blow the socks off of Wall Street investors.

The plan took me two weeks to create and was two-hundred-plus pages filled with color diagrams, cost, and PowerPoint animated slideshows. While I cannot say I did the most important financial part of the plan, I will say my contribution to the technology plan did assist with winning the funding. Within weeks, a new financial processing firm was born with $250 million in funding capital. As promised, Mr. D and Mr. F made me the chief information officer / executive vice president with stocks and partnership. All I could think was, "Wow, I hit pay dirt!" This all came with a large executive corner office, custom furniture, and the option to work from home.

In just a few short months, I learned more about the responsibilities of the top-level executive. Since the business was brand-spanking-new, there were many aspects of the business simply missing key components. We were missing many of the basic components such as a company logo, copiers, chairs, office space, and checkbooks. We were pretty much a multimillion-dollar company with nothing in place. To make matters worse (but absolutely amazing), we closed our first multimillion-dollar deal in record time. As a result, as the technology officer, I was tasked with coming up with a technology plan to bring on 1,200 new employees in nine locations around the country with a new corporate office in Philadelphia. With many nights of no sleep and extensive technology-design sessions in my basement, I was able to make my mark in the financial industry and deliver sound technology platforms in record time. In approximately two years, the company had grown to twenty locations around the United States, three locations in Canada, and multiple banking relationships. I was hobnobbing with bigwigs all over the place and considered a bigwig myself. First class was my mode of travel, and there was tons of travel in the two-year period.

I met hundreds of other executives in other banks, credit-card companies, investment banks, etc. I traveled to Ocean Reef, Florida, for fishing trips on yachts and enjoyed excellent hotel arrangements at the Ritz Carrolton and St. Francis hotel in San Francisco. We had arrived. My wife and I bought a new home along with a couple of new luxury cars. We were saving money for the first time. At this point, I seriously cracked the glass ceiling and was well into the six-digit salary. I was making all sorts of positive changes to the family lifestyle. In summary, my wife and I began working on a true financial plan to get our lives in line with our overall goals. My two sons were two years old and two months old.

After a few years of pure enjoyment, things changed. Our CEO, Mr. D, was replaced with a new CEO who was from Napa, California, where diversity is only a word in the dictionary. In a matter of a few months, the only two black executives (another colleague and me) running the two major areas of the company were moved under (made subordinates) our white counterparts in a smaller subsidiary company. All the other changes that followed only benefited the company Biffs and Buffys. After being the pioneers and brains behind making the company what it was, by a simple change in the upper top-level executive management team, we were no longer respected or valued. The only people impacted with the changes were black, and the company eventually moved to Napa Valley where traditional top-executive purity was the motto and standard for the new executive team. Mr. D was also very surprised about what occurred and also moved on. As executives, we received some compensation; however, it was nowhere near the multimillions we were due in the long run. Racism is a hurtful thing.

I am sure that some of those who are reading this book will think I am weak for not doing as the Biffs would do and fight, or take them to court! Well, everyone needs to understand that going to court as an individual against a company is a bankrupting endeavor. The company always has more money and will most likely not run out of it before you do. However, not willing to easily step aside from what was rightfully mine, I entertained the Equal Employment Opportunity Commission (EEOC). In the scope of it all, I learned the EEOC is not equipped in handling such complex executive-level issues. As a matter of fact, I found people at the EEOC to be cold to the issues I was describing, and at one point a representative from the EEOC said to me, "What are you complaining about? You are a rich young black dude. What are you complaining about? We have people with real issues." I understood there were others making a lot less money than I with unfair-treatment issues going on; however, the thought that my case was less important because I was an executive making an excellent salary was an unacceptable and deplorable response from the EEOC representative. I helped launch a company, which today is worth over a billion dollars, and at the time of my termination, my stock was valued by the ex-CEO to be worth twelve million dollars. I believe if I was treated unfairly, it was because I was black, and others obtained wealth and related benefits they did not deserve simply because they were white. The EEOC turned out to be a cold organization and a complete waste of time. I was not personally funded enough to survive the cost of a straight lawsuit and was forced to take what they would give me and walk away.

In the end, taking the chance and launching the financial processing company was still well worth the rewards I received. The money went a long way and allowed me to set up my family for a great lifestyle and position me for possible early retirement. When the dust cleared, I was back to square one and dealing with videoconference interviews, tests, odd meetings, and more companies with very little diversity at the top. I think the biggest lesson learned in getting involved with such big business deals was the role of lawyers. I had no personal historical reference point when we launched the financial process and obviously missed key issues associated with the legal aspects of the deal to properly protect me. My recommendation to myself in the future is to always have an attorney review all legal documents associated with new executive employment or business deals. You need serious legal firepower behind you for total protection.

Taking the leap to start your own business alone or with others is a serious step to take and is "well worth the risk" if you should choose to move in that direction. However, it's a very busy road, and you must be capable of wearing many hats. If done right, the upside is in your favor financially. I personally plan to launch a business sometime in the near future because of the overall cumulative benefits. However, for now, I am equally capable of making an excellent salary and benefits operating as a top-level executive.

CHAPTER 8

Statistics: The Soul of the Company

The Internet! What a wonderful tool. By the time I moved on from my first CIO position, the Internet had fully matured. Information was at my fingertips, and I now had more tools to combat my lack of information about the companies I was applying to. In 2001, the dot-com bubble had burst, and many companies had a fear of technology. Most companies still needed technology executives; however, they wanted people who were supersharp and could control the technology at the hands-on level.

This all seemed great. While I was out of the company I helped start, I was now capable and qualified to investigate executive opportunities in Fortune 500 companies. My quest was very difficult, and many of the same tactics existed to show a bias toward the black executive candidate. I remember at one meeting, I was flown to Atlanta from Philadelphia and picked up at the airport by a stretch limo with breakfast waiting in the car. The company had a full day planned with at least eleven people for me to interview with. Our phone discussions were detailed, and everyone discussed on the phone their interest in me and my extensive background in technology which they were trying to implement. The day was outlined with lunch at a local restaurant and a trip at another local company data center. They even had their HR department send me a preliminary executive term sheet with actual initial numbers of a possible deal included. My interview was around nine o'clock, and I was in the lobby early, ready to go. For approximately thirty minutes, I sat directly in front of the receptionist on the lobby sofa as a number of people came out and talked to the receptionist. I went to the receptionist and asked for my contact and was told she was in a meeting. What nobody knew was that my contact requested another HR rep to get started with me since she was going to be late from her meeting. That person turned out to be the company recruiter (flunky) that initially contacted me by phone after viewing my resume on an internet executive job site. A few minutes later, a tall skinny white guy came out with anger in his voice, saying, "When Mr. White gets here, tell him we will have to reschedule. He probably got caught in the traffic." I heard his comment and said, "I am Mr. White! I have been sitting out here for over an hour and watched you walk by repeatedly." I told him that if he was looking for first-time candidate, why not ask, "Are you Mr. White?" He immediately told me, "I saw you sitting there, but I did not think you were Mr. White. I'm sorry! I was expecting someone else." I told him he should have only been expecting a male in a suit, and that's what I was wearing. What else was he expecting? It became clear to me that he was not expecting a black man and just walked by me again and again without considering the possibility I might be black (in downtown Atlanta). Once again, my power resume and deep, "well-spoken" phone voice confused them.

During the mild ruckus, the receptionist called my contact, who immediately came out. I could hear the receptionist say off to the side, "This candidate was totally ignored by your recruiter. He assumed the candidate was white and left this nice black guy sitting for an hour." (The receptionist was black.) After the realization of what was going on, the rest of my day at the company was just noise. My contact at the company tried to apologize, but as we toured the facilities, I noticed again diversity was nonexistent at the top management level. Needless to say, I never heard from them again!

Finding a job is hard enough, but finding an executive job as a black man is extremely tough. After all the hard searching, I found my next opportunity at another bank. I entered this multibillion-dollar bank as a chief technology officer / senior vice president (within a subsidiary). The bank was interested in launching a new company within the bank scheduled to generate billions in revenue. For a higher total overall annual compensation package in salary and bonuses, I agreed to a $50,000 cut in base salary. The bank was so large at an international level it was difficult for me to determine their diversity through online research via the Internet. When I arrived at the bank, there was no technology team in place for the subsidiary company we were starting. I put together a team of twenty-eight people, and together we changed the dynamics of the bank. Our systems allowed the bank to expand into mortgage securitization via a risk-managed process. Monthly volume went from six hundred million per month to $2-$3 billion of acquisitions and securitizations per month. During my first year, my team and I developed new platforms, installed a full data center, coded multiple applications, and passed all internal audits. Regardless of the company's success, our bonuses were weak, and recognition for our efforts was nonexistent. Other platforms, of smaller scale, headed by white managers, were pumped up regularly. My technology division was later migrated into the bank's standard global technology organization (no longer a new company launch), and I became a "generic line director." With even more success the next year, my team and I again received lackluster bonus compensation as our efforts generated hundreds of millions for the company. Now in my third year at the bank, I understand the statistics, and I kick myself for not taking the time up front to gather the data I needed. Throughout the bank, over the past three years, I have only seen two other black men at my level. According to the intranet information, at the managing directors level (top-level executive with colossal benefits), there are 1,027 managing directors worldwide, and of that number, only four are black. To make matters worse, none are black women, and the most recent hire of the only four black managing directors was in 1994 (it is now 2004). The fight is in the statistics. When you examine the corporate ranks across the country, it has become acceptable to have such poor diversity statistics (at least in terms of black Americans) among top-level executives. Working as a senior vice president or director is excellent compensation. However, working as a managing director in a $350-billion-dollar bank opens the door for high base salaries, stocks, and multimillion-dollar bonuses. With statistics like these in place today, I do not see myself ever becoming a managing director with my current employer.

With the functional abolishment of affirmative action, these types of statistics are just fine with the government and most employers. Some say the best joke the devil played on God's children was convincing everyone that he did not exist. I believe another big trick played on black people was to get us to accept the classification of "people of color." When you talk to companies about diversity, they statistically tally all nonwhite males and total all the heads and call it diversity. However, as with the bank I am with today, that mixture of diversity includes everything with a very tiny percentage being black. Walking around the bank, I observed there are a number of Indian managing directors, Chinese managing directors, and white female managing directors. Companies have found a way to diversify as a part of their well-publicized diversity program with every nationality (race) except black at the executive ranks and still report excellent diversity statistics.

I do not center my life and career direction based on these statistics. Overall, low statistics concerning blacks among the executive ranks is and has been the norm for many companies. It's good to see companies trying to improve the situation with diversity programs; however, I doubt true results will be shown across the board with the absence of true affirmative action. I am sure it is possible for affirmative action to be abused when not properly managed. Affirmative action, being a government program, is no different than any other government program, which on occasions has mismanagement issues (i.e., Department of Defense $100 hammer-purchasing program, Medicare, Welfare) However, to suggest that there is no need for affirmative action because companies will police themselves, America is kidding itself, and we as black people have serious troubles ahead.

Standing on Fair Ground

I'm sure there are many people out there who want to suggest affirmative action is tied to what happened to blacks during slavery. In short, the general feeling is slavery was a long time ago and "white America" has long since paid its debt to minorities (specifically blacks). Even though slavery was over a two-hundred-year running saga of injustice implemented by America against blacks, we do not have to talk about slavery to understand why racism still exists today and how equal opportunity is still decades away. For example, as with African Americans, Jewish people experienced massive atrocities from 1933 through 1945 (estimate) as a part of Hitler's death camps during the Holocaust. Still today, the pain and sting of what occurred to many Jewish families

produces pain and sorrow across the country. This pain is a type
of pain and anger Jewish people have a *right* to feel without having
to deny what occurred as a part of their history. As African
Americans, we have to pretend slavery is now a nonissue because
it was a long time ago. Examine the facts: Jewish people and all
of America today openly discusses the Holocaust as something
Jewish people "survived," which makes them a strong people.
Sadly, the Holocaust lasted twelve years and killed more than six
million Jewish people, and some fifty-nine years later, it is fresh
in the minds of many Jewish people and all of America. Slavery
occurred over a period of two hundred years. Given the viciousness
we know occurred through the time of slavery, I can only imagine
how many blacks died over such an extensive time span. The
reason the details of what happened to the American Indians is
not reviewed every year along with the details and atrocities of
slavery as we do each year with the Holocaust is simply because it
happened here. Yes, in order for black people to celebrate what
we "survived" for two hundred years, we have to also point the
finger at the country we also live in and love so much. That alone
makes the whole notion un-American, and therefore, the country
goes on not recognizing how a two-hundred-year struggle
becomes a woven thread in the soul of the people impacted.

In terms of discussing affirmative action, we can leave behind the
issue of salary for the simple reason that slavery cannot be
discussed. Since slavery is not up for discussion, let's bring our
struggle up to more recent times and streamline the context. For
example, as a relatively young black person, I don't need to
reference issues related to slavery to pull on the pain of the African-
American struggle. During the '50s and '60s, blacks were being
hung and denied rights as all of America watched videos of violence
against blacks on their TV sets all across America. Stories like
Emit Till's murder in 1955 were happening all the time just some

forty or fifty years ago. If America can accept Jews still feeling the pain of their atrocities, which occurred in 1943, America will also have to come to grips with blacks still feeling the pain of what occurred throughout the '50s and '60s. I raise these points only to say that as time lines go, images of blacks being sprayed with fire hoses and bitten by police dogs as ordered by a white governor was only a short time ago. It is illogical to assume a few years of affirmative action have eliminated such racial attitudes and solidified equal opportunity for all in this country.

The reason the federal government monitors corporations so closely concerning taxes and white-color crime is because if the honor system was used, taxes would never be collected and theft would spread like a disease. As you can see, even with the laws, corporate theft and tomfoolery still occurs. I find it illogical to believe that the federal government does not trust companies to do the right thing concerning their *obligations* with taxes, but the same government, when it comes to human rights and fair employment, will trust those same companies to exercise fair hiring programs and diversity programs as it relates to civil rights of minorities where today there is no penalty. Before affirmative action was instituted, the ratio of black and other minority executives was low. During affirmative action, the ratio of black executives was low. Now that affirmative action is gone and companies "believe" they do not have to adhere to any type of racial-balancing federal regulations, you can expect corporate "preferences of comfort" to continue in this arena and smoke screens to cloud the room in order to mask the true composition of corporate America at the executive ranks. If you have access to the Internet, if you have a job, or if you get an annual report, take some time to look at the pictures as time goes by and see how "openly" the company you are reviewing or working for is actually practicing diversity at the executive levels.

CHAPTER 9

The Black Executive, White Women, and Black Families

Many affluent black male athletes, musicians, lawyers, doctors, and other high-powered professionals very often have white spouses. How does this happen? Is it wrong? Why does it make black women so disheartened? I am addressing this issue not to spark turmoil, but because I have been privy to many conversations with black men, black women, white men, and white women on this issue, and I have my own opinion based on what I have come to understand over the years. Overall, this discussion is about the type of women (white, Asian, etc.) connecting with affluent black men and its perception and impact on the black women. The reason I am focusing in on white women in this discussion is because of the angst seen on the black woman's face when a successful black man is with a white woman.

In short, a number of black women are angry about this particular interracial marriage because they would like to be where Buffy is! I don't believe most black women care about the issue of interracial marriage in the overall scope of things. I think the primary issue is when it occurs with *high-profile* black male executives on a recurring basis. I believe a poor married interracial couple is viewed as a nonissue and is overlooked with no more than a simple comment such as, "Damn, how did they end up getting together?"

Just like black women, black men grow up with extensive images of beauty being white women. When we read our magazines and go to the movies, the preponderance of females being presented to all males as the object of our desire is the white woman. Most TV commercials present beauty to little girls and boys using white women. Yes, we have women like Halle Berry, Gabrielle Union, and Queen Latifah being offered here and there, but for the most part, we all see mostly white women presented as the figure of beauty by the media. After a period of years, the image of beauty becomes white. Most rich men on television and the movies are chasing white women, big houses, and big cars. That all said, there is still the issue that black men growing up usually know very little about white women, but when we come into money, somehow we end up with white women all around us.

As a child, all of my black male friends and I dreamed of being rich and successful and flaunting our success with the perfect new luxury car. We never saw BMWs or Rolls-Royces in the hood; however, the constant presentation of these cars in magazines as being the "mark" of success drives us to immediately seek and purchase one of these cars once we become successful.

When a black man reaches the rung on the ladder where he is making $200,000 plus bonuses and more, I can pretty much guarantee you that the women running in his new circles eight hours a day at work and after work, in social events with the company, are not black. At this point, we are constantly meeting with tons of young white women. If you do not see many blacks at the top of corporate America, you cannot expect a busy top-level executive's day to be interlaced with meeting black women. I remember watching an episode of Punk'd on MTV, and the boys from a young successful black rap group were on the show. While everyone watched to see how these guys were going to be punk'ed, I watched the setup and activities in their average day such that everything seemed normal to the young rappers. These rich young black rappers were invited to a pool party with all young white women who were all over them. Somewhere between hormones and just plain volume of presentation, these young black kids were all hyped up with interest in these white women. This is how it happens! Even during a joke, the lure for these young rappers were white women. Just like corporate America, white promoters determine who attends the parties with our rich black artists, and sooner or later the odds take over, and they are hooked up with a white woman.

Now what is missing in my analogy? Well, what is missing is where the black women are while this is happening. The black women are there all the time at church, night clubs, and many other locations. However, "history" between the two sexes causes all the problems. Since I am a black man, I will describe how black men feel we are categorized by black women.

While we have many flavors of black men, in the end, black women see us as a brother (black man going someplace), a "playa", or a stupid ass thug. The typical black man feels the first absolute second spent with a black woman is your only chance to be categorized. If you land in the wrong category, it's over! You have to be careful with your approach as a black man. Where driving your BMW is your sign of doing well, at first glance the BMW-driving black man can be perceived by the black woman as a playa. On the other hand, wearing the wrong clothes could make you a thug or something worse. Whatever the case, it's not often that the black man is assumed up front to be a "brother going somewhere."

Without any conversation taking place between the black woman and the black man, the categorization has taken place. This is the "history" I spoke of earlier, which makes it less complicated for the white women to become very attractive (accessible mentally and emotionally) to the rich black man. I call this categorization by black men and black women *virtual DNA*. Virtual DNA is what every black woman uses to examine a black man before she can determine which type of brother he is during the early stages and initial meeting. It is the "attitude" we give each other that destroys all opportunity in the relationship. We feel we know each other so well we can spot a playa, a corny brother, a sucker, a mama's boy, a skank, a freak, and a gold-digging black person a mile away. Fact of the matter is that the use of virtual DNA is why black women today feel they are tired of black men and black men are tired of black women. I believe there are bad apples with all men and women, but the virtual DNA baggage we carry specifically against each other is killing our black relationships.

Virtual DNA has become so extensively present in the black woman-black man relationship that verbal communication channels are no longer trusted. For example, sometimes purely based on how a man dresses and how a black woman executes her facial expressions, black people are making relationship decisions to move on. Meaning, "I was talking to her, and she rolled her eyes," or "Don't you know he had the nerve to be wearing this thick gold chain?" I am sure both issues seemed important at the time, but it does not mean she is a skank full of attitude or he is a player only trying to tap that (you know what). Virtual DNA has to be removed from the dating process between the black woman and black man, or there will be more and more single and alone black people.

Now let's bring it home. How does a white, Chinese, Japanese, Filipino, or whatever woman find herself enjoying the lavishness in the home of the black male executive, rich athlete, or musician?

First, it is important to understand that the infatuation with white women is particularly sexually strong for some black men due to the historical bombardment of images, which makes them a natural fantasy to the black man, along with the jump-off fantasy for white women concerning black men. It is at this point the virtual DNA kicks in. Since the black man has no virtual DNA connection with the white woman and vice versa, they can only see each other as a true "possibilities" and allow things to work out, not depending only on what occurs along the road of courtship. As a matter of fact, the white woman simply looks at the gold chain at the level of quality and says, "That is a nice gold chain," and when she rolls her eyes at him, it looks cute. Before you know it, Buffy and Kaheem are getting married. Buffy is driving a Range Rover into her four-car-garage home, and some black women call Kaheem a sellout.

Overall, I personally believe it is possible for anyone from any race to fall in love and get married. However, I am a black man and have been through all the DNA reviews with black women. I felt that many times with black women I had to prove myself extensively to justify a basic hello and continue a conversation. Before I could get to hello, I had to make sure my hair, pants, shoes, walk, and car were in line. There is such a thin line between "possibility" and "playa" that some black men would rather walk down a different racial street to see what the differences are. For example, when I was at the supervisor / assistant-manager level, to many black women I knew as associates, I was a playa-type brother because I was making a little money (a bit more than other black guys in the shop) and was probably only after "that thang" and had no plans beyond pleasing that booty. The bottom line was that some of the other black men in the shop were in fact only after "that thang," and by association of the work, I became a part of the "men after that thang" group.

Guilt by proximity was very difficult to banish with my female associates.

I remember in 1987 I was traveling all over the United States as a director of business development and technology for a National Mortgage Association. While on travel, I gave a speech to an audience of three-hundred-plus people in the mortgage industry. During a private presentation, I had a white-female "basic instinct" moment and immediately thought, Wow! After the presentation at dinner, this same white *Vogue* cover girl vice president came toward me and was so intimately friendly. She had a lower position than I did in the scope of it all and was making less money, but she had no virtual DNA in the mix. If I had not grown up in a hardcore black lifestyle, I may have gone for her very forward advances.

Later that night, there was a buffet dinner for many mortgage bankers, and I saw a young black woman about my age and decided to sit at the same table. I figured, hey, I just gave the primary speech at the conference; she has to know I am about something. Well, to my surprise, I hit professional virtual DNA just by sitting down. Apparently, she signed up late for the conference and missed the opening speeches. She had no idea who I was, and even though I was in a suit like all the other white males there, she gave me no idol chitchat based on typical industry dinner-party courtesy. She spent the rest of the evening laughing loudly with a number of Biffs and Buffs at the conference. Two days later, I had given my second speech at the executive table, and I saw her a few rows back. After the speech, she came up to the executive table, talking to me as if we were chummy for the entire conference. By that time, my virtual skank DNA was triggered, and I blew her off without a second thought.

Two years later, I hit the virtual DNA again. In 1989 I drove a black Hyundai Excel with a car phone and did not smoke or drink. I quickly became a corny suit-wearing black guy driving a cheap-ass Hyundai trying to front with my car phone. I met women who, without realizing it, told other women I knew that I was a corny guy walking around in suits, trying to front but couldn't because I could only afford a Hyundai. Some of these same women would drive down to Haynes Point in Washington, DC to parade themselves around the park looking for what I can only assume would be "quality black men." Without ever really having a serous conversation with any of the women, virtual DNA had done me in. In a nutshell, I bought a Hyundai because the dealership was within walking distance to my apartment and it was all I needed in the DC area. I took the subway most of the time to work, and I was saving my money to buy a home. Finally, I had the cell phone (which was very expensive back then) because I was starting a business and was missing too many calls at home, which, by the way, was a very nicely furnished one-bedroom apartment with a fireplace, balcony, and no roommates. By looking at me on the surface (a mistake made by most young black women and men), virtual DNA did not allow these women to take time to understand I was an assistant vice president in technology making $45,000-$60,000 a year and had no wife or kids and was still well under thirty. What black women called corny, white women call smart and diligent and would approach all the time. Naturally, I cannot say all black women are like the ones I met any more than I can say there aren't a number of fronting brothers out there. But somewhere along the line, the virtual DNA has to stop to simply give people (both black men and black women) a chance. During this same time period, I met a black woman who had plans for the future as I did and let go of her virtual DNA as I did. That woman is now my wife of thirteen years.

As black people, we need to kill the virtual DNA and start talking again. I am sure couples will still determine they may not be compatible, but if the virtual DNA does not stop, we will see more black men marrying other women without defined virtual DNA (i.e., Indian, Asian, Chinese). Not that there is anything wrong with marrying women from other races, but virtual DNA is a silly reason for black men not to be connecting with black women.

Black people have enough battles in this world to deal with and should not perpetuate the use of virtual DNA and other negative information thrown around that create an atmosphere where we are battling our better halves. The key to improving our relationship is not getting comfortable with the rhetoric being communicated. For example, the more statistics we hear about black single-mom families, the more black women look at the situation of being a single mom as "somewhat common these days" and no big deal. This feeling ties into other comments such as, "All the black men I meet are either drug dealers, out of prison, going to prison, gay, or players." When you examine the whole package, all this negative information make the black man a villain and allows more black women to feel the black man is not worth seeking as a mate.

From slavery through the 1960s, there was a reason that black people made it through the struggles. We were tight all over. We had black churches filled to capacity, black families growing through tough times, and a true sense of unity that was able to shake the halls of the United States legislation to change our destiny forever. The fight is not over. We need to ignore and reject the statistics pounding the airwaves every day and rebuild our families with a feeling of what a family is and what it takes to struggle together through the ups and downs of what we experience each day. To dispute the negative connotations, I know many black men who have never been to prison and are very much capable and ready to join in the daily struggles of black married family life. As a black man, I can unequivocally make the statement that there are far more black men *capable* of *unbelievable success* than there are black men given the opportunity to realize that success without first being forced to undergo serious emotional, spiritual, and financial breakdown. Black men and black women are a necessary partnership needed for survival. Doing this alone is an unbelievable struggle.

CHAPTER 10

Me and Mr. Jones

W̶e all know the stories.

- I was the son of a sharecropper.
- We grew up in the projects.
- We moved on up to the east side.

Whatever the story, we all know what it takes for most black people to move up from being poor, low-income, ghetto, or whatever it is you want to call it. In the end, if you are lucky enough to break through and live some level of rags to riches, it will be virtually impossible to avoid Mr. Jones. In poor and low-income areas, we grow up with our parents dreaming about hitting the number or winning the lottery and becoming rich. We sit around the dinner table, talking about all the things we would buy and do "if we hit the number." Since the people doing the dreaming are living in real poverty, the dream of what would be done if wealth was actually realized is not a joke. Life in America is filled with many Americans and immigrants dreaming of the good life. The good life is different for everyone. If you were born rich, the good life is about more profitable investments, real estate, and exotic vacations. If you were born poor, the good life is about a much-better home that's yours, a good, working, expensive-looking car, new furniture, and money in your pocket.

As you make your way through the various levels of middle to upper incomes, you will face the demons of keeping up with the Joneses. This is a particularly lustful lure, which almost always brings down most families (black or white). It is very easy to tell rich kids to be less materialistic when they get good jobs and access to high salaries. It's easy because rich kids do not long for nice homes, pools, cars, and good pocket cash. They grew up with these things and most likely have them through high school and college. However, poor black kids making their way to the top have many more pipe dreams and yearnings. Poor kids who get access to $50,000-plus salaries at a reasonably young age will quickly see those things they have dreamed about all their lives as pending purchases. They will buy the BMW, Rolex, and other such items. At first the purchases are to satisfy their own personal need to get what they have missed all their lives. However, make a few more dollars and the issue changes. Before you know it, the need to have what others have becomes more of a driving factor, and this is where most crumble and come to live a paycheck-to-paycheck lives.

On many occasions, I have known black friends who get better jobs and immediately buy bigger and more expensive "things." This cycle continues for years until one day they realize they are credit rich and cash poor. They have a few hundred thousand dollars of debt, expensive cars with extremely high car notes, and very little money in the bank as savings. Before they know it, they are simply working to pay bills, and the only way to improve the situation is to find another job and make more money. Many people who "move up" versus those who grew up with the silver spoon end up in this situation. When you get a taste of the money, you believe you can have more than your worth. Credit purchases become easier to make, and before you know it, you are just fronting the good life during the day and struggling as a family at night. The scary part of this mathematical equation is that if anything goes wrong, bankruptcy becomes imminent very quickly. The first thing to go is the home; the next thing to go is college savings (if there was any), and finally, if you are not totally broke, your pride is totally shot as you head to your second job on the bus.

As a black executive, you need to examine everything you have going on. If you have no other rich family members, you need to always have cash in the bank to get your family through during hard times. While you have a yearning for the material things you have dreamed of all your life, you need to learn to buy what you can afford while saving for the disaster at the same time. As with many black families, there are only a few breakout family members with high-paying jobs or successful businesses; therefore, we only have a few family members (if any) to tap into if something goes seriously wrong. We cannot live as black executives by overextending and trying to be more than we are. We also have to recognize the fact that we may not be at the top for a long time, so doing the right things with our money will be key to not being poor again.

The first demon we need to deal with as a black executive is the car demon. If you've never owned a luxury car, you may not be aware of the fact that the typical car note for a $60,000-plus luxury car is $900-$1,200 plus per month. In some areas of the country, that is a mortgage payment. You have to learn how to deal with the flashy car demon somehow, some way. When I first became a true executive, I purchased a Lexus LS400 using my stellar credit. I had no problem making the payments of $800 per month; however, I noticed I was saving less because of it. I later scaled back the car to an Acura RL and today an Infiniti G35. Yes, I can afford much, much more, but in the end, why bother right now? I can do better things with the money. When

I was buying my first single family home, the loan officer told me and my wife we could afford a $700,000-$900,000 home. I told the loan officer the four-thousand-square-foot home in a new construction development subdivision for half that price was just fine. At the time we purchased our home, I was at the height of my rising salary. There was a strong yearning to "prove" to Mr. Jones how well I was doing, and I almost made the $500,000-plus home purchase. After some serious family discussion, we decided not to purchase the much-yearned-for dream house and purchased an excellent home in an excellent neighborhood and school district. For the rising black executive who came through the ranks, I too had to beware of the purchasing demons from my childhood. These demons could break you as an adult.

Getting rid of the demons compelling you to keep up with Mr. Jones is an ongoing process. You will find yourself looking at new homes, watches, private schools, cars, in-home technology, the bomb landscaping, and many other very expensive material things. I remember when I was a senior midlevel executive at a large bank and just getting to know a number of other executives in my industry sector. I remember going to a technology conference and spending a lot of time with a few colleagues. Along the way, I learned that one guy (Biff) purchased a $600,000 home, but the down payment came from his mom and dad. In addition, his family paid off his student loans and bought him a Mercedes 300E. When I returned home and began learning more about my neighbors, I learned that the young woman across the street (Buffy), who was single with a small child, was given the home she was in by her father who was the builder of the multimillion-dollar suburban complex I was living in. I came to find that many of the people at work and in my new neighborhood were doing well through birth or had funds they could tap into at any time. My situation was different; hard times for me and my family would remain hard times for us until we could resolve it. We had to learn the difference between our situation and their deep family wealth (support system) through family ties. There was no comparison. It was impossible for us to play the material possessions game with the Joneses.

As a black executive who realizes that opportunities for me at the top are far and few between, I, along with my family, had to create a plan to combat the possible of not remain above the glass ceiling. Our goal was to attack the major bills in support of issues with the income later as companies struggle with giving top-level executive opportunities to the black candidate (me). I am forty-two and on a plan to pay off most of the mortgage, streamline auto notes, and save much more cash in the next three to five years. My plan is to have no bills, bank my high salary and bonuses, and ensure easy college and postcollege support for my kids and our retirement.

As a black executive, you need to make sure you plan and only live within your means and you can control your destiny. Getting sucked into a credit-rich life creates the illusion of living the good life, but it's just a matter of time before that bubble will burst.

Everyone needs to learn how to deal with serious financial problems when things change. For example, imagine you are making a great salary, and all is going great. You are a top-level executive; your salary has your family in an excellent financial situation, and you are enjoying many of the things in life you dreamed about. When you reach this status, you need to establish two types of emergency accounts. The first is a large emergency account simply to cover critical family issues. The second is an account with enough cash to cover all your expenses for a minimum of six months, preferably one year. In most cases, up-and-coming black executives do not have financial family support systems. The typical black executive may be the only one in their family with such financial success. Remember, it will take the average black executive much longer to land the next position (black staff is thin at the top), so having emergency accounts are vital to maintaining life before draining other primary accounts (i.e., checking, savings, kids' college mutual funds). If you find yourself out of work and halfway through your emergency accounts, you need to immediately begin moving toward reducing the material commitments. Do not try to hold on to the house, luxury cars, etc. If you don't make a change soon enough, you will find yourself broke, under foreclosure, and in a sad state. In the end, these are all material goods. Yes, it will hurt to take a step backward, but if this should ever happen to you, you will survive without total bankruptcy.

Chapter 11

Help Me—Hurt Me

Help Me:

The most difficult battle in climbing the corporate ladder is family. When you begin this journey, you will spend a bit of time on par with siblings and other relatives. However, at some point in time, you will surpass the national average in annual income and soar beyond what others in your family could possibly imagine you are banking. For example, making a base salary well into the six digits along with significant bonuses will turn you into the "help-me man." Meaning, everyone will assume you have money to help them. I have been living this for ten years now with various relatives. Ten years ago, when we had our first child, my wife stopped working and left her job as a human resource manager at a large national department store chain. While this was great for our family overall, the house, cars, kids, and all the expenses quickly reduced the wonderment of the paycheck. Initially, on the surface we were saving a bit less, but with my wife becoming the family's full-time CFO, the tax plan was maximized along with the overall savings plan. It was at this time that my wife and I slowed down the spending and took a look around. We were living quite nicely and decided to stop upgrading. As a result, we are in an excellent place today. Some might take a look at my wife and say she is a housewife, and what is that? Well, what people fail to recognize is when you have the money to allow one spouse not to work, they have the opportunity to investigate other avenues of interest for other moneymaking ventures or personal growth. Very few people get that opportunity in life, and the day I become a house husband and obtain the same opportunity my wife has now, I plan to take it. While I love what I do, over the years I too have acquired expertise and interest in areas outside of my core expertise, and like my wife, I would love to act on some of those opportunities. For now, it is about making money and building the piggy bank to allow both my wife and me to become a house couple in early retirement, pursuing other fulfilling objectives in life.

On the downside, when you streamline your finances for future plans, you quickly come to realize that you no longer have indefinite funding to continue helping people regularly. For example, when relatives call and communicate they need help, it is never for $100. It is for much more, and after ten years, it has become a bit much. Over the past ten years, I have paid mortgage bills, electric bills, corrected teeth, and funded years of monthly AOL use. If I were to have any financial problems today and needed help from relatives, there is nowhere for me to go. Most are getting by, struggling, or doing bad and can barely help themselves. This is where the mental anguish comes into play. In the bank, I have funds that can help my relatives; however, to extract these funds, I would destroy the financial plans for my own family. As much as it hurts to begin saying no, I had to start. The guilt is tremendous, but I have been through hell and very high waters to get to where I am, and perpetually giving everyone money is not a part of the plan and eventually would corrupt my personal family goals and objectives.

Handing out cash is sometimes a good thing, but other times (when it becomes a repetitive process), it may be better to teach a person to fish rather than giving away the fish. If you're in a tight family, it is very difficult to see others in your family not doing well even after you make various financial contributions to assist; however, you also have an obligation to yourself and your family to continue moving forward. This was one of the most difficult issues I faced in my struggle.

Hurt Me:

Personally, I feel I should be further along in my executive goals. I may or may not reach the megaexecutive level in the near future, but overall, it's no longer necessary or the burning desire it once was. I am in a good place financially, my family is happy, and my skills and facilities are intact. I have the option to think about another crack at my own business, and God willing, I have the time. I expect I will land either a CIO, CTO, or managing director's position again in the future. I believe it is possible, and I suggest that if you are a black executive going through what I am going through, hang in there, and you will prevail.

Unfortunately, the squashing of affirmative action makes it easier and more acceptable for bias practices to hurt blacks in the workplace. The larger issue I see today is companies being layered with young white executives from top to bottom. Diversity is practically nonexistent, and even if affirmative action were to resurface in the form of a new law, corporate America now has embedded new young white executives who will be in those positions for years to come.

On more than one occasion, the policies were so lopsided and racist my team of white employees came to me and said, "I really thought racism did not exist anymore, and my eyes have been opened! I would never have believed some of the things I saw happen to you if I had read them in a book or heard through rumors. What I find crazy is that I am stuck because you are stuck, and I feel like I now know somewhat about how it feels to be black. This is just crazy." I will remember those words and that moment for the rest of my life because for the first time I realized that others saw the unfair practices of corporate America against black men and black women.

Shortly after the white members of my staff made these comments, we got into deeper conversations. I explained to them the issues they see are daily. I told them about the time my wife and I went into a Mercedes, Lexus, and Volvo car dealership and watched how whites who entered the dealership were greeted with smiles and assistance while we walked around for minutes and had to convince someone to help us. As black Americans in such dealerships, we were seen as window shoppers, not buyers. We left the dealerships and drove someplace else to make our purchase. I also explained that when I attend technology conferences as a black executive and walk the conference floor, when I enter a technology booth, I get no attention. Whites are immediately approached when they enter the vendor's booth, but I have to find someone willing to take time out from "other conversations" to help me. They do not assume I have the power to make decisions and spend money. When I leave these conferences, I make it a point to remember such vendors.

As I continue my struggle, I am learning much more about the total impact of unbalanced employment and promotion policies and practices in corporate America. I can only hope and pray things will get better.

JOURNEY-PLANNING
COOKBOOKS

An Introduction

Building a career is like creating a new gourmet dish based on an unknown, complicated recipe. You try a number of ingredients, temperatures, and spices and hope the meal tastes delicious when it's done. During my journey, I documented some of the spices and various temperatures I used and tried to create some personal planning cookbooks to help others successfully complete their own journey.

While some exceptional people such as singers, Olympic athletes, and painters begin honing their craft as early as age four, the general population typically begins plotting their life journey in high school. When I started my journey in high school, the idea of "being successful" someday was exciting, and I made a conscious decision to document as much of the trip as I could for the sake of passing it on to whoever wants to know. Twenty-four years later, I find myself a little bit battered but still excited over the trip. I have experienced some good times and some bad times over the years and believe what I have learned (regardless of how small the tidbit of information) will help others approach and evaluate the journey at a higher level of understanding.

During my journey, I realized much of my journey was based on two key principles that I used as core stepping stones to plotting a successful future. *Principle one* states, "While life is comprised of many, many experiences, there are some core 'chunks' of our lives that define who we are and where we end up in our lives as a result of those important chunks of experiences." *Principle two* states, "The small decisions you make along the way in the end may overshadow the big decisions you thought were life changing but actually were not." The journey-planning cookbooks are based on three "chunks" of core areas that are critical to your journey and the little things we make decisions on along the way that are far more important than originally thought.

As I walk you through each of the phases, some aspects of the planning will seem passé; however, please read the information carefully. Each phase has unique detail that seems consistently to elude many in the black community slowing our growth and progress. The first phase, from a black perspective, of critical importance was high school. Overall I did well in high school; however, the importance of my time in high school did not become clear until after my high-school graduation. The second chuck was the multifaceted aspects of attending college and absorbing all of what is available to absorb. While I did well in college, the importance of my time in college did not become clear until after my college graduation.

The final chunk, from a career standpoint, was planning to become an executive or entrepreneur. This was the most complex phase of my life for many reasons. While I mastered the art of the deal and getting the job without taking any prisoners, all of the other factors occurring at the same time made this phase complex, full of side roads, fraught with spiritual beat-downs, and layered with racism. As you add love, marriage, and a baby carriage, before you know it, the complexities of this phase of life will challenge you to the marrow of your bones, but if you plan the best you can, you can easily survive it.

The primary purpose of the journey-planning cookbooks is to provide early insight to my readers in support of my favorite statement, which is "if I knew then what I know now." Utilize my journey-planning cookbooks as mini-step-by-step guides which provide "extra" information you may need to consider as you embark upon your personal career journey. The major decisions will be obvious; however, as I said, the little decisions also have the ability to change the course of your overall results. Use the cookbooks to examine key issues I found critical in my journey, which I believe you will face as an African American in your journey.

PERSONAL COOKBOOK

The High School Years

The high-school years, when forensically examined, brought out some very interesting issues once documented and compared later in life. In this planning cookbook I cover issues that seem small in nature but are valuable after high-school graduation, as well as key "deal-closing" issues that must be addressed in order to move to the next step and be taken seriously. In my family, we are still dealing with the handful of relatives who make it into college and still a much chosen few that actually graduate. While in college, I watched many of my friends leave for reasons such as lack of maturity, homesickness, lack of finances, and poor study habits. High school (or prior to it) is the time to deal with these issues and obtain the tools necessary to truly prepare for the future.

Prelude to the Details

The tragedy of my experience as a black kid in high school was the limited focus placed on the importance of the overall experience beyond the fact that you had to attend and graduate. Since my days of going to high school, the same old song was being sung about inner city schools not being given the funding required to properly provide a quality education. While this is unfair, the problem is perpetual and not going away. Until that time comes, parents *must* fill in the gaps to generate success or final support to fill in the gaps. In between the two parents not making enough, two parents working two jobs, single parent, welfare, or whatever the situation is, *parents must fill in the gaps!*

If you're not sure of what the gap is, the gap is the experience we all have as black adults and the *true* passing of that experience to our kids, making sure each child does his/her job to properly move on the next step. The typical black student coming out of an inner-city high school will take all the minimum classes and do very little else beyond the requirements. Most extracurricular activities for black students usually relate to sports. We are either on the sports team or just going to the sporting events. To most black students now and in the yesteryears, high school is all about getting through the classes, hooking up in the lunch room, working after school, and meeting up with friends after work. As adults, we have all come to learn the impact of a poor high-school performance on our adult lives. We have all come to learn that high school, as trivial as it seemed to us at the time and to your kids at this moment, will define our lives for years to come, and there is no "do-over."

Like everyone else, I tell the same post-high-school story. While I was in high school, the so-called kids who had it going on all did poorly in school (the cost of being cool). Today, most of those same guys and girls are poor, still in the same neighborhood, loaded with kids, dead, or in jail. The interesting part of this perpetual churning pot is that while I was in high school I just could not imagine a life this bad for simply not doing your school work.

As a parent, you have to nag your kids about their homework, projects, extra activities, and planning. The schools are under no obligation to ensure your kids a graduation or satisfactory report card. The school's responsibility is to present the curriculum and move your kids to the next period. It is your kid's job and yours as a parent to push them when it seems too hard, nudge them when it's boring compared to going to the mall or down the block, and comfort and inspire them when they have studied as hard as they can and only got a C when they wanted an A or B. You also need to teach them to professionally challenge subjective grades (i.e., English papers, history papers). Inspiration and communication can go a long way, and considering how defining high school will be on the rest of their lives, it is worth all the extra hassle you may have to go through as a parent.

THE JOURNEY-PLANNING COOKBOOK SPECIFICS FOR HIGH-SCHOOL SUCCESS

Focus on the serious principles concerning success in math and English.

I cannot stress how important it is to understand the core principles of math and English in going forward in your lives. If you basically skated through to the ninth grade and you are not the master of multiplication, fractions, subtraction, and division, you need to nail it down now. On the summer before you go into the ninth grade, do whatever God, the school system, your smarter friends, and your parents will permit you to do in order for you to master basic mathematics. For example, if you don't remember long and short division such that it is a nonissue to perform the calculation, get it done. If you cannot recite your multiplication table with confidence, learn it now. As you move through the ninth grade and the rest of your high-school years, all other math (i.e., algebra, trigonometry, geometry, and possibly precalculus) will crush you simply because you have not mastered your basic math skills. This may sound crazy, but not too long ago I went into a convenience store, and the cash register was broken. The clerk behind the cash register could not manage the cash or calculate change without a calculator. The reason we have these issues today is schools and parents must do more to *drill* kids on these subjects. The new school environment today focuses more on light drilling concerning the raw mathematical process and deeper drilling on passing state exams. Both can coexist; however, good support will have to occur in the home. You do not need a computer to take care of this task, a few boxes of index cards and a pen will do just fine.

The principles of English are exactly the same. Year after year, you have taken test after test on nouns, pronouns, adjectives, and sentence construction. However, when questioned by surprise, many barely remember the various English principles of speech or the written word and their properly use. Learn it now! Again, on the summer before you enter the ninth grade, get it done. English and math will be the two single subjects that operate in cumulative fashion from high school through college, and allowing yourself to move from grade to grade with a weak understanding will seriously hamper your college career or plan to become an entrepreneur.

Before I leave the English topic, I need to address "Ebonics." Ebonics is the biggest joke perpetrated on black people since allowing us to become grouped into the category people of color (which I will address in another cookbook). In short, society giving poor street language a name seems to have given millions of young black kids some low-level stamp of approval to speak like an idiot. If you travel the world, many people speak English. A student having to learn proper English is not about trying to be white; it is about being able to simply communicate in a global society. The United States is not unique in subdialect speech. Other countries have language-dialect issues, but when it comes to the language of communication, you must speak it properly, and when they are taught to speak English, it is proper English. Other countries will not accommodate their culture to the language of Ebonics. Therefore, blacks following the lead of those who support Ebonics as a language and support such nonsense will create a generation that will not be able to communicate nationally and globally. As a black man, I recognize we have a cultural language, and we can speak that league to each other at times that are private, in our music, in poetry, and between friends. However, to head into a job interview (or any other professional situation outside the cultural group) and use Ebonics as your language of choice is foolish and idiotic. Please, go to school, learn English, and speak English!

GOALS FOR HIGH SCHOOL: BIG THINGS AND LITTLE THINGS

Many high-school students truly dislike the fact that parents and teachers try to force career choices early in high school. In all honesty, I agree it is difficult to know what you want to do for the rest of your life in the ninth grade. With that said, what do you do?

I am not trying to scare anyone, but it is important to understand your first year in high school is an important and critical year. This is the year you to set the tone for the next three years that follow. While you may not know exactly what you want to be in the future, you can at least make a decision to graduate from high school with the best possible grades and interpersonal skills. This is also the time to get to know your teachers, who will become crucial to helping you prepare for next steps after high school. Being successful in high school is all about growing intellectually, academically, and emotionally in four years such that you are capable of moving away from home and managing your life as an adult. In order for this metamorphosis to take place, you have to create and understand the idea of setting goals and objective by planning. Some of the planning principles for high school are the following:

> Say *no* to anything that is not good for you and the goals you have made for your life. Begin to be your own person and build your own plan. Start with saying no to drugs, smoking, and alcohol. It will seem *extremely* cool at the time, but in my lifetime, it brought early unemployment, herpes, AIDS, cancer, liver damage, and death to my friends and acquaintances. These things are killers, so saying *no* will go a long way for you to have the most satisfying life you can have.

> Say *no* to cheating. Today, we live in a very technological society with gadgets galore. Do not fall prey to using this technology to cheat. Many have tried and found themselves severely punished and tarnished for life. Cheating also makes you dumb. Very few people would like to have a surgeon operating on them who cheated on exams and doesn't really know the details of the operation. While his test scores may look great on paper because he cheated at times, you run the risk of death as a result. The information you are taught in high school and college can be called upon at any time in your life, and cheating will not truly prepare you for your future. It prepares you for definite failure in the long run.

> Focus on obtaining the best education you can through hard work, studying, and asking for help as soon as you realize you need assistance.

➢ Create consistent habits for studying, completing your homework, and finishing projects. Become proficient with computers. During class, practice taking good notes on the material being presented. The art of good note taking will be needed for the rest of your life. This is very important!

➢ Speak up in class. Don't be a face in the crowd. By speaking up in class, you begin to overcome the fear of speaking in public, which I still observe in adults forty years old and older. This is very important in college and as an entrepreneur. Overcome this shy trait!

➢ In class, don't be afraid to be wrong. Many times kids will not speak up because they feel they have the wrong answer, so when the teacher asks, "Does anyone want to try," the room goes quiet. The reason the room goes quiet is because most other kids are also afraid to ask. This is a good chance for you to "lead" and not be a "follower." You will come to notice others will follow your lead and become interactive with the class. They will begin to look up to you as the person willing to *do*! This is where leadership begins.

➢ Begin keeping your old test materials for later review for the finals. This simple practice could possibly increase your final grade by an entire point since your tests are critical references when the final approaches.

➢ Expand your communication lines beyond your friends. Recognize your teachers as people and friends who have information that could be valuable in helping you get to the next level.

➢ Begin understanding what comes next. Talk to people about careers; read up about college and its requirements; participate in high-school activities in addition to sports. Try to get on a first-name basis with your guidance counselor, principal, and teachers.

> When the time comes for the ACT and SAT, prepare one year in advance. If your family cannot afford to send you to prep classes, get them free from the library or buy the prep books out of any store and begin practicing. These tests are very important, and you should not perform poorly simply because you are unfamiliar with the structure of the test. Find out now how much the prep classes cost and discuss with your parents a 360-day plan to save the money. Use the Internet as much as you can on this and other issues. Also, begin searching for money early for college.

> At the end of each summer, use the last two weeks to begin waking up your mind and rid yourself of the summer brain haze. Start reading a novel that sounds interesting and reviewing your English and math from the previous year. Wake up your brain!

* *Special Note on Finding Money for College*

Finding money for college can be like participating in an Easter egg hunt in an area the size of an airport. The first step to finding funding for college is reading up on the process at least two years in advance. Execute this process in four ways:

1. If you are a soon-to-be parent and you somehow found your way to this book, start saving for your kids' education *now*! Regardless of the amount, the goal is to save whatever you can each month and use "automatic" transfers from your bank account if you can to ensure it actually happens. Waiting too late to begin saving makes this goal more and more impossible as time goes by. Before you know it, hitting the lottery will be your only option, and we know the

odds of that happening. The key to any long-term savings plan is "time." Use time to your advantage when saving for college or retirement or in buying a home.

2. In the summer after your tenth-grade year, get the *Newsweek* annual edition of *"Sending Your Kids to College"*. This magazine issue comes out each year and will serve as an excellent resource for updated information on the topic. Also, buy the best book available on college financing from any local bookstore. The book will provide more detailed information and concepts beyond what the magazine will have to offer.

3. Use the Internet! Go to key sites such as *www.fastweb.com*, *www.collegeaidresources.com*, *www.scholarships.com*, *www.collegenet.com*, and others you can track down by using good search engines such as *www.google.com*, *www.yahoo.com*, or *www.lycos.com*. What you are searching for is city money, state money, money from the college, government money, industry scholarships, small and unique funding, unique scholarships, job-related money, etc. For example, the daughter of a fireman may have access to local and national scholarships offered only to kids whose parents are public servants. You need to get deep into this process and fully understand that *information is power*. The less information you have, the less power you will have to help fund your college education. Immerse yourself in this process.

4. Begin talking to your teachers and guidance counselors at least in the tenth grade. Let them know of your intentions and tell them you want to pretend you are going to college next year (while you are in the tenth grade) and go through the full information college process; fill out the forms (do not mail them) and understand the deadlines. Have them dump all the financing options they know of on your lap; bring it home. Document this process well and put it away for safekeeping and later review.

5. Talk to parents who have already gone through this process (recently), and have your parents do the same. If you have a friend who has an older sibling in college, talk to their parents about the process. Have your parents do the same at work.

When searching for college funding, hit all resources. Execute this work early so that you know what to do when the time comes. College money is like a financial melting pot. There is cash out there for poor kids, rich kids, kids with good grades, kids from poor areas with bad grades, kids whose parents are government workers, and kids who have a focus in computers, art, or whatever. Earlier in my career, I became a licensed stock-and-bond broker and focused on helping people save for long-term goals. So many times I met black people asking me what they can do for college to help their fifteen-year-old teenager have a better future. My nicely presented answer to them was "hit the lottery." The bottom line is saving for college is a long-term process. When saving for college, the key is to *start saving early and save regularly.* When saving for college or your retirement, the first thing you need to do whenever you get paid (i.e., regular paycheck, bonus, lottery hit) is to pay yourself first. This means since you have eighteen years to do the best you can for your graduating high-school senior, you must make each month count financially. You should acquire a level of guilt if a month goes by and you did nothing (even $25) to help your child pay for college.

To better understand the numbers and why time is important, think about this:

Example 1
A monthly savings of $25 for eighteen years with no interest is $5,400. With interest, it may be $8,000. A student going to an

in-state school where the cost is lower could use the college savings calculated for at least one or two semesters along with a few Pell Grants and student loans to make it to graduation.

Example 2
A monthly savings of $50 for eighteen years with no interest is $10,800. With interest, it may be $18,000. In some colleges, this is payment for the full four years or a good supplement.

Example 3
A monthly savings of $100 for eighteen years with no interest is $21,600. With interest, it may be $30,000.

To better understand which savings vehicle is best (i.e., mutual finds, 529 plans), read magazines such as *Money* magazine and *Smart Money*. Also, use the Internet! Time is the blessing God has given you to plan for your kids. Saving a little at a time to take a big step for your child is far more important than the beer budget, a new large-screen television, or other less-important items. If you are a teenager reading this book, stop asking your parents for products like $150 sneakers and expensive clothes. Help them fund your college education and stop asking for dumb things.

I have already stated the importance of math and English. All other classes are about learning the work. Therefore, work hard to learn the work and make a point to yourself to allot the time to study properly and do well. The other important issue is communication. As a high-school student, you need to branch out and put yourself in situations where you are working with adults such as teachers and community leaders. This interaction will improve your interpersonal communication skills and prepare you for life after high school. During your high-school years, you "must" get involved with those so-called corny activities. These activities might be the chess club, debate club, Future Business Leaders of America (FBLA), etc. Since my original focus was to become a lawyer also, during my high-school years, I was also a member of the national mock-trial society, where high-school students pretended to be lawyers and compete nationally to become the best high-school legal team. When applying for college, college recruiters like to consider students who can do more than just put their head in a book and pass a test. Colleges "hope" the students they admit will someday become leaders, and leaders have a habit of doing more than the minimum. Get involved in high school!

If you or your child follows the basic plan above, life after high school will be more in line with your high-school training, and you will be better prepared for the next level. It is very easy to do less and hope for the best, but most people who put in less than their best usually get even less than they expected. Remember, you cannot redo high school. Have fun but take it very seriously.

Having our black children practice these principles with *enforcement* from parents will have a profound effect on the future of black America. Last week, I went to an executive meeting, and we were all talking about our high schools. Most of the white men and women around the table were talking about a number of people who have moved on as attorneys, doctors, computer developers, and other such careers. My part of the conversation was short. Many of my high-school friends are not doing well and fell to the harshness of the real world right after high school. Their weak grades prevented them from moving on to college, and their inadequate speech and understanding of how to move forward left them poor with two-bit jobs no more than a few miles from home and the old high school. Let's teach our kids early the value of school and what to do to be successful. Start today with your kids or a kid down the street. Make it happen!

Special Note about Educational Assistance

As a father today living in an area where elementary schools and high schools win state blue-ribbon awards, I realize black students need a sound process for obtaining assistance. As your child progresses through school, the first and most important thing you have to learn to say is, "I don't know," and get help for your child. Many parents simply don't help their child because they're not proficient with basic subjects such as math, English, and science. Also, many black parents in low-income neighborhoods (once they realize their kids are having problems) do not secure actual assistance. I understand working two jobs may be tiring, and possibly having a basic education makes it difficult, but if your child needs the help, you have to make it happen. The competition that low-income black kids face with other students around the country is amazing. During my school years, I do not remember a single friend or any other black student being tutored. I find this amazing since many blacks drop out because of failing grades. I also know of many black students that dropped out of high school or failed most tests all the time. What black parents need to know is that tutoring needs to become a part of the plan. Without it, some black students will fall behind and never catch up. For example, I currently live in a class-A school district where the average family income is approximately $100,000 and up and there are tutors being utilized regularly to simply sharpen the child's skills. In many cases, I see third graders with regular tutors, and these kids are obtaining a level of intelligence beyond the normal public-school curriculum. Black parents who are not willing to do what is necessary to ensure support for their kids on this front will watch the gap widen between their kids and other kids around the nation.

In low-income areas where teaching and schools are said to be subpar, it is important to work with tutors if that is at all possible. I believe all kids are smart and that intelligence needs to simply be turned on. Sometimes it takes extra work for the switch to flip on. Talk to your kid's teachers and school administrators for more information on such assistance and use online support such as AOL School or AOL Homework help. There are more options available for tutoring than you may tap into, but it takes research to find the right answer.

Not Planning to Go to College

As much as I believe the new global competitive world we live in requires as much education as possible to survive financially and obtain the best future you can, I also realize some high-school graduates may not want to go to college. If your choice is not to go to college, you should consider some key points.

The first point you should understand is that if you are a decent high-school student and you aspire to attend college but you are not ready, consider working first for a year or two, and then go to college. Over the years, I have met a number of people who were not ready for college after high school and simply waited. They eventually graduated college on a time frame that worked best for them.

The second point is to determine if you do not plan to attend college at all. If this is your path, you should examine long-term opportunities. For example, unless you graduated from high school with special skills and a killer resume, you will be on the bottom rung of the pay scale, looking to move up in the future. You will be the person in the mailroom who works his/her way up to the executive office. You will be the entrepreneur who started a company at a young age and turned it into a profitable company or possibly an empire. Whatever your story, you should not assume you will walk into any company as a junior executive with high-paying salary. Look for companies that will offer you a career path, training, college reimbursement, health insurance, retirement planning, and dental coverage. If your goal is to begin building a career, you need to get yourself into a situation where you can take care of yourself and become an independent tax-paying citizen. If you don't know which companies might offer you such options, a good place to start is, for example, the *Fortune* magazine and its list of the "50 Best Companies to Work For." Track this information down online first by going to *www.fortune.com* or *www.fortune.com/fortune/diversity*, which lists the best companies for minorities.

I always suggest anyone taking this path immediately take the civil service exam after graduating from high school. There are many government jobs out there for high-school graduates at the entry level, and each is most likely a long-term opportunity with room to grow and the necessary benefits. Government opportunities cover multiple areas such as administrative, finance, technology, agricultural, and many other fields. The goal, if possible, is to put yourself on a path as quickly as possible that will allow you to become independent, pay your bills, grow, and move yourself to the next level that works best for you. The government needs good people also, and this has been a great option for many people over the years at the local, state, and federal level.

Personal Cookbook

The College Years

The college years are an interesting period. Somewhere between the open environments, no parents, access to alcohol, sex, and on-campus activities, the college student has to still find a way to succeed in the semiannual goal of getting good grades. The immature high-school students entering this environment will not survive.

One of the primary reasons I saw a number of my black friends drop out of college was their inability to be mature in college. The lack of maturity I am referring to is not the crazy college stunts regularly shown on TV and the movies. While attending college, I met people who did some of the craziest and wildest things I have ever seen; however, they were mature enough to still focus when necessary to maintain an A or B average. The maturity level I am discussing is related to young kids leaving home and not knowing how to handle the independence. Not only the independence of taking care of themselves, but also how to handle college business-related issues that frequently occur. As a high-school student or parent of a high-school student, you must utilize the last two years of high school. You must allow your kids to grow as young adults by letting them do such things as washing, ironing, and sewing their own clothes, getting up in the morning without constant prodding, and other such issues.

You should involve the high-school student in the business of running the house. Have your son or daughter sit with you when paying the bills, or let him or her call the gas company when something goes wrong or occasionally purchase all the groceries, etc. The most important issue to include the high-school student in is working with adults other than their teachers. These skills will build their ability to deal with college administrators, manage conflict, purchase goods and services, not destroy their clothes when washing and ironing them, and manage what little money they have. Treat this period as "basic training" for college life. Struggling to deal with these issues as a freshman will take the focus away from quality studying and will make the freshman become counterproductive during the all-important first semester.

Students and their parents should not take the induction into the college environment lightly. The abrupt disconnection of parental and hometown relationships could seriously impact school work. To deal with this, if possible, parents should accompany their kids during check-in and hang around for a few days. Parents need to get a feel of the area and better understand how their kids will be living. As kids plow their way through college, they should utilize the Internet to communicate via e-mail, instant message, and instant message with videoconferencing (if available). Services such as America Online and MSN have these services fully integrated as a part of the service. During the early stages of college (first two years), I do not recommend that students get their own credit cards. When possible, students should have debit cards in their name but under their parents' control or replenishment when funds run low. Getting money to a college student by debit-card management will provide on-time financial support and avoid the high use cost of services such as Western Union. At times, the college student will find a need to go shopping for life's basic necessities such as deodorant, toothpaste, disposable cameras, tube socks, and sneakers. To help with these needs, let your fingers do the walking by using the Internet! If you need to put together a care package for a college student, go to sites such as *www.cvs.com* for toiletries and *www.walmart.com* and *www.amazon.com* for many other nonperishable items. Depending on the area of the country, online sites such as *www.peapod.com* will also allow you to send perishable groceries to the student.

Each year, the college student will face new and sometimes unique challenges. If you are a parent that didn't attend college, you need to know that your student will need help. The more you communicate, the easier it will be for students to communicate needs and for parents to pick up vibes when something is wrong.

Another strange but important fact about freshmen entering colleges and universities is the issue of bacterial meningitis. Before you or your young adult leaves for college, call the school and speak to the health department and obtain the latest reports on bacterial meningitis reported at the school. If necessary, call the state health department. Bacterial meningitis is an infection of the fluid around the spinal cord and brain that causes flulike symptoms, including high fever, headache, and stiff neck. It's sometimes called spinal meningitis. Bacterial meningitis can be fatal, and you should get the vaccination if necessary. It is my understanding that because college students have a tendency to run on empty due to late studying, partying late, and part-time working, their odds of their weakened systems contributes to their susceptibility to contracting bacterial meningitis. While I was in college, I heard of at least three students who contracted bacterial meningitis, and it seems to become more widespread over the past few years. The best suggestion here is "the best day starts with a good night's sleep."

All college students need to remember how important sleep is to good heath and well-being.

Feeling behind the Curve

As an attentive high-school student in Yonkers, New York, I now know the difference between my high school and the high schools in the neighborhood where Buffy and Biff live. The quality of education is not the same around the country, and once you hit college, that will become evident. In a number of cases, black students find themselves in first semester remedial courses to deal with English and math shortcomings. Sounds familiar; take care of this in high school as I stated in the high-school cookbook. As a student at the University of Maryland, I found myself in the remedial situation, not because I did not do well in high school, but because the depth and detail of what I learned differed from Buffy and Biff's education. Meaning, I learned algebra at the surface level (how-to), and Biff learned it at a methodology level (how-to and why). There always were at least twenty-five kids or so in my high-school class (if not more), which was constantly interrupted with fights, student tardiness, and a shortage of books. On the other side of the coin, Biff enjoyed orderly classes of fifteen students and a tutor at home and no after-school job. Trust me; the difference in the end is profound in two major ways. For example, when I landed in college, I had no knowledge of short division. My elementary school, middle school, and high-school training taught me long division only. When I saw short division after high-school, it was like a new and foreign process. While this was the college situation, my solid base in math and English allowed me to fill in the gaps quickly. Another example is time lost. For example, on average I would say it took ten minutes for my high-school classes to settle down after all the initial classroom antics. If you total the time, the ten minutes per day in six primary classes is sixty minutes of total learning loss daily. That number, if fully analyzed, averages out to 1,200 minutes per month which, multiplied against ten months out of the year, is a total of 12,000 minutes. This means, in layman's terms, our kids are losing an estimated two hundred hours of learning each year simply due to the impact of other students and uncontrolled classroom management. Before I move on to the cookbook, I should state that I went to the University of Maryland, which is a predominantly white university. While I chose Maryland for its curriculum and its location, I also chose Maryland because it represented the "vision" and epitome of what a college or university was supposed to look like. I believe that in the end, most colleges and universities offer similar benefits to the students, and the right student will move on in life successfully if his/her studies are taken seriously and with conviction. Over the years, I have met Ivy League graduates and trade school graduates on both sides of the spectrum. Meaning, I have met Ivy League graduates doing nothing special and making decent salaries while at the same time going into some companies where technical school graduates have risen to the ranks of chief engineer with commanding $120,000-plus salaries. The bottom line is that getting the diploma from whatever school is step one; doing something with the diploma is step two, and much of that success is based on personal vision, aggressiveness, risk taking, and prayer.

The first point to remember about college is you are on your own. College is not a place where someone will wake you up for school or care if you completely miss classes. Black students need to always remember college is not free, and the only business at hand is getting good grades. Any student not willing to put the proper time into studying with conviction should consider putting college off until he/she is willing to make the personal commitment. In college, there is always something to study unless you are a natural genius. If you find yourself watching all the TV shows, going to all the parties, kicking it with your girlfriend or boyfriend on a regular basis, you need to examine your grades. If your grades are mediocre, the odds are you need to change your priorities and dedicate more time to your studies. The one misperception many new black college students have is the idea that they have four years to graduate from college. This is not true. It is important to understand that each and every college and university has a reputation and status related to quality to uphold as an organization. Meaning, any student with a consistently poor performance will be *expelled* from the school. Most institutions of higher learning will only allow a student one poor-performance semester without question. If a student performed poorly for two consecutive semesters, the student will be placed on academic probation. If the student is unable to improve his/her performance, the student *will be* ejected from the university. Once ejected, you will be required to pay all outstanding bills and student loans since you cannot prove your status as a full-time student. It is very important to begin college with the drive and goals to do your absolute best.

BEST PRACTICE: STEPS TO ACHIEVING COLLEGE SUCCESS

Studying hard is a well-understood plan for college success, but there is so much more below the surface that can impact college students and divert their attention and focus from their primary objectives. The list below outlines some of the external mental pollution always present and impacting the prepared and unprepared student:

➢ Obtain a driver's license as adult identification before your first day in college. It is your sole proof of identity, *and* you need to be able to drive just in case you find yourself with college friends who are drinking and trying to get behind the wheel. If you cannot get your driver's license, at least get a formal, state nondriver's photo license ID. As an adult, you should never walk around without some type of acceptable photo ID.

➢ Keep track of when key college forms are due. This is not your parents' responsibility. You need to communicate to your parents issues from the school concerning application submission, Pell Grants, and other such financial management issues.

➢ If you need a job, try to quickly get an on-campus job by discussing it with school representatives during the college-induction process. Tell anyone and everyone you meet while visiting the college you would like to get an on-campus job. If you drag your feet, you will miss out on all the easy on-campus opportunities such as working in the library, ticketing cars, working in the bowling alley, or working as sales clerks in the student union. It's much better to work on campus as a student. Working off campus typically means working for a company less compassionate about student issues and higher travel expenses.

➢ Get to know all you can about the college process. Talk to seniors and to friends already in college. You need to understand all the facilities such as test centers (places where students look at previous tests for the same period concerning a particular class and professor), TAs (teacher's assistance), syllabus (standard class outline for the semester), and pass/fail classes, and when to do this. There are tons of "deadlines," "steps," "options," and "processes" in college. Get familiar early in the game. For example, I learned about

the University of Maryland STAR Center (test center) in
my senior year, which was a major resource for white
students for four years to obtain previous tests sorted by
professor.

➤ Nail the first semester: Remember that your entire time at
college is driven by your grade point average (GPA), and
this is a cumulative process. The best way to have a good
college career is to have a near-perfect first semester (straight
As). Meaning, if you can put off calculus for the second
year, do so. If you can spend your first semester taking
only the required 101 classes, do just that and *nail* those
classes with As and Bs. This high GPA score up front will
help you in moving forward. If you have to take much-
harder classes because of your declared major, take the least
amount of classes you are allowed to take, and do your
absolute best to *focus* and *nail* these classes. A poor
performance in your first semester will cripple your moving
forward. It is *extremely difficult* to push up a low cumulative
GPA once it's on your record and part of your overall
calculation. Remember, the classes only get harder, so
banking on getting an A at the next level of a class you
received a D in will be a much more difficult task than you
can currently imagine.

➤ Be organized. Keep all your tests and quizzes, and correct
all incorrect immediately after it's graded. This will give
you a good final-exam study template. If you simply bring
home an exam marked 80 and never get the correct answers,
you will have a poor collection of material to refer to during
the finals.

➤ Get help immediately when you realize you are not picking
up on any of the material or concepts.

➤ Follow the exact same outline I gave you for high school.
Practice good study habits and note taking.

➤ Get to know your professors, and don't be a number on a list. College professors are your highways to credit and paid internships later in your college career, and you will need references.

➤ In your sophomore year, begin planning for postcollege. If you are two years into engineering, begin looking for good employers and asking professors for contacts, suggestions, etc. You will find some of the opportunities you may seek will require a year or so to prepare, and starting early will provide you the necessary time.

➤ A year before you graduate, obtain one of the easy-to-get credit cards in your last semester. Obtain an American Express and a Visa or MasterCard, and use your home (back home) address; however, do not use them. Tell your parents you have the cards, and work out a plan of use. Meaning, if you need something like shoes, ask your parents and then use the card. They should pay the bill as soon as it comes in, or you pay the bill if you have a job. The goal is to put some activity on the cards and pay them off in full immediately. Doing this over a six-to-twelve-month period will put you in good standing before you graduate and prepare you for life after college when you may be trying to use the cards for your first major purchases after getting your first job. You also need good credit to get an apartment without a cosigner.

➤ Take lots of pictures even if you use disposable cameras. If you do not, you will regret it. Also, get the "back-home" address and phone numbers of your college contacts, friends, buddies, etc. Once you graduate, they may be impossible to find. If you have the back-home info, Mom and Dad will always know how to reach them.

In the end, your job in college is to get good grades and graduate. If possible, try to have fun during the ride.

PERSONAL COOKBOOK

Planning to Become an Executive

Unlike the state-required plan to graduating high school or the four-year plan you get in college to graduate in prelaw or engineering, there is no such plan for becoming an executive in corporate America. If you are reading this chapter because you want to follow my cookbook for becoming an executive to make tons of money, you need to clearly understand there is "no such cookbook" or formula. In your quest to become a black executive after high school, you need to focus on four key principles and issues related to family values:

Principle 1: Learning never ends. The more you learn, the more confident you will be with your skills and industry expertise. Never stop learning or think you've reached a point that you know it all. Change is constant, and you must keep up with changes in your family, perspective, business, occupation, career, and personal goals through periodic reassessment. Your learning should include getting comfortable with the types of financial information that drives and controls businesses, as well as managing your own personal finances. In short, you need to become comfortable with understanding the right and left side of a balance sheet, as well as reading and understanding a company's annual financial report. This may be work you need to complete after college on your own. Not all majors in college teach students about the financial system of a company or of personal finance/economics overall. In many cases, someone majoring in engineering, architecture, or biochemistry never learns anything about financial company management in college. However, each could find themselves, fifteen years after college, on the executive track with no background in business or personal finance. Overall, I recommend taking college classes to obtain this information; however, there is always room for good reading material to get you started. My recommendation for software tutorials would be Financial Competence, which offers inexpensive corporate finance and personal investing computer-based training material. Their product can be purchased at www.competencesw.com or by calling 727-298-0341. Books I recommend are *Understanding Wall Street* by Jeffrey B. Little, *The Wall Street Journal Guide to Understanding Personal Finance* by Kenneth M. Morris, *Reading and Understanding Annual Reports: A Guide for Investors and Businesspeople* by Edward Fields, and *The Guide to Understanding Financial Statements* by S. B. Costales.

Principle 2: Be respectful while being direct and forceful with your colleagues, partners, and superiors in business. You must always remember you were not hired to be "just a warm body." Most companies hire you because of what you know or what you can do for their company. Present your expertise and be willing to deliver the bad news when necessary.

Principle 3: Always know whom you work for and what they do. Do not operate in your functional area without a clear understanding of the primary goals and objectives of the company. Whenever you land a new job, learn the business of the company. If the business is insurance, learn the details of the insurance business. Keep abreast of the news associated with your company.

If you ever find yourself working a few years for a company and you are not fully aware of what they do, whom they service, and what the profitability of the company is, you are not on an executive track or executive material.

Principle 4: Always know your endgame. You should know why you are working so hard, looking for a new job, trying to purchase a house, or setting up mutual fund. Unless you believe in the *Forrest Gump* principle of haphazardly moving through life, you need to know where you are trying to get to. If you don't know your endgame, you will have no idea of what to ask for, apply for, turn down, or create. If you don't have a plan, you will most likely miss opportunities and goals. I understand everything cannot be planned, but as they say, "Fail to plan, plan to fail."

As you make your way through the various rungs of becoming an executive, keep track of everything you have done in your career. For example, over the years, you will receive many performance reviews, which are in writing. You should obtain a copy of all those reviews and keep them in your possession. As time goes by, companies will merge, fold, or totally be repopulated with a new set of employees. These documents will help later in your career as you try to explain what you have done and the kudos you received along the way.

Family Values

Family and self! It is important to *understand* and *identify* how decisions made will affect your family. If you are married, decisions should be joint and most likely in the best interest of everyone in the household. The life value I am about to discuss has to do with a "relationship" that either grows or falls apart as a result of an executive life. During the quest to become an executive, you will first find you have no time for yourself. You will find yourself capable and being asked to work without breaks. You will realize this phase is under way when you feel months and years going by out of college without memorable vacations and happy times to heal your soul. During your quest, take time out for those breaks. Enjoy life and let the company wait. They give you vacations, fifteen-minute breaks during the day, holidays, and sick days. Take them all. Use that time to infuse your soul and for personal goodwill. I did not do this, and as a result, I sometimes burn out quickly as an executive and "need" time off. I also constantly wish I could get that time back. The next point on this topic is about your spouse if you decide to get married. Just like you, your spouse needs a break from work, kids, and the daily grind of life. Find time to get away when possible.

Finally, we have those wonderful kids. Time is the key to getting the most out of the relationship between you and your kids. All the important feelings and connections between children and parents must be earned. Much of what has to be earned such as love, respect, caring, sharing, and countless other feelings, is best learned by example. Because you are an executive, the company will make countless attempts to make use of the time you've set aside to build a strong relationship between you and your kids. While it is OK to attend some corporate events and conferences, do so with a work life balance. Once you blow the quality time with your family (especially your kids), you cannot perform a do-over. You can quickly become a virtual tenant in your home with your kids showing you very little love and respect. You will not get what you do not earn! The best reference I can offer is a song by Harry Chapin titled "Cats in the Cradle," which was originally recorded in 1974. The album (CD) is titled *Verities and Balderdash* and was released on Elektra Records. I listen to "Cats in the Cradle" regularly as a reminder of what happens when we are there but "absent" in our kids' lives.

AUTHOR'S FINAL COMMENTS

My final comment is about perception. *The Glass in My Throat* is a type of autobiographical review of my early life experiences, as well as a snapshot of my work history. I have been through many situations while trying to become successful at a level that is satisfactory to me; however, *The Glass in My Throat* does not include much of the information that describes the good times in my life. While growing up, my brother and I had tons of fun as kids in Yonkers, New York, just playing basketball in the dirt yards or whatever we could figure out to have fun with. He has been my best friend for years. My friends from elementary school are still my friends today, and my college roommate and I stay in close touch. Most of all, I am having a great time with my wife and two sons with a goal of taking my kids to all fifty states before they graduate from high school. The best thing about enjoying your life is that making the decision to enjoy it is up to you. If you let the crap going on at work make its way into your family life, you will have poisoned the only antidote available during those times when your work life struggle really brings you down.

The purpose of *The Glass in My Throat* is to outline, for African Americans, the challenges associated with managing the stages of life and becoming an entrepreneur or corporate executive. The challenges are real, and you have to be tight in your presentation and professional game. As I said in earlier chapters, your personal survival begins in the hood, but your professional journey begins in high school. We as black people must learn to plan better for ourselves and our kids. The plans must be executed and not just talked about on BET and in black newspapers and magazines. To become a black executive, you must learn to remain calm and *think* your way through the many situations you will face. You must be able to deal with the details and understand the financial aspects of the job as you learn to manage people, processes, strategies, groups, and divisions. I do not want anyone reading this book to think racism is present in all companies. It may be, but I cannot confirm such a statement. What you have to examine is what you see when you walk into a company. If you hear a company has been in business for over fifty years and there are no blacks to be seen outside the mailroom or supervisory level, you have to question why there is no diversity. Each year, thousands of black students graduate from undergraduate and graduate colleges/universities, law schools, medical schools, and technical schools all over the country. We are out there in record numbers professionally, and somehow the executive opportunities are extremely difficult to secure. I have found the opportunities are out there, and I have participated in the interview process, but somehow in the end, the hiring stats favor Biff and Buffy. In each job I lose or never get called back for, I usually determine who they hired by calling into the company and asking for the person in the position I interviewed for. In each case, Biff or Buffy landed the great new job.

Finally, I would like to say something about "being given chances." I have been very strong about my position concerning the limited number of blacks at the superexecutive level. I personally believe the statistics concerning diversity at the top levels of most companies is absolutely pitiable. However, please do not walk away feeling all white CEOs, chairmen, and such are all prejudiced and racist. Such a statement is not true, and it would be totally unfair to paint such a broad brush against any group. The fact of the matter is that each opportunity I received to move up the ladder was given to me by a white person who obviously was able to look beyond the color of my skin and realize I had something much more to offer professionally. I like to believe you earn your reputation as a company and as an individual. A company with no diversity at the top executive levels year after year and does nothing to offer such opportunities to others have made a decision on the mixture it "prefers" in its top executive staff *and* is proud to show it off to the world (i.e., annual reports, Internet management presentations, and news articles). As African Americans, we have to continue to try to push through these barriers, not lose our faith along the way, and continue to enjoy life during the struggle. In the end, the glass we get in our throat today will make it possible for our children to take the elevator to the top-level executive suite without all the issues and drama. Perseverance is the key!